STRATEGYMAN

VS. THE ANTI-STRATEGY SQUAD

USING **STRATEGIC THINKING** TO **DEFEAT BAD STRATEGY** AND **SAVE YOUR PLAN**

RICH HORWATH

GREENLEAF
BOOK GROUP PRESS

Published by Greenleaf Book Group Press
Austin, Texas
www.gbgpress.com

Illustrations, cover design   Nathan Lueth
Coloring   Samantha Somers, Nathan Lueth
Interior, back cover layout   Sunny DiMartino
Editorial support   Agata Antonow, Annie Rose Stathes
Project management   Keli McNeill, Yolanda Knight, Kristin Westberg

Distributed by Greenleaf Book Group

For ordering information or special discounts for bulk purchases, please contact Greenleaf Book Group at PO Box 91869, Austin, TX 78709, 512.891.6100.

Publisher's Cataloging-in-Publication data is available.

Hardcover ISBN: 978-1-62634-640-6

Paperback ISBN: 978-1-62634-549-2

eBook ISBN: 978-1-62634-550-8

Part of the Tree Neutral® program, which offsets the number of trees consumed in the production and printing of this book by taking proactive steps, such as planting trees in direct proportion to the number of trees used: www.treeneutral.com

Printed in Canada on acid-free paper

19 20 21 22 23 24   10 9 8 7 6 5 4 3 2 1

First Edition

GREENLEAF
BOOK GROUP PRESS

TABLE OF CONTENTS

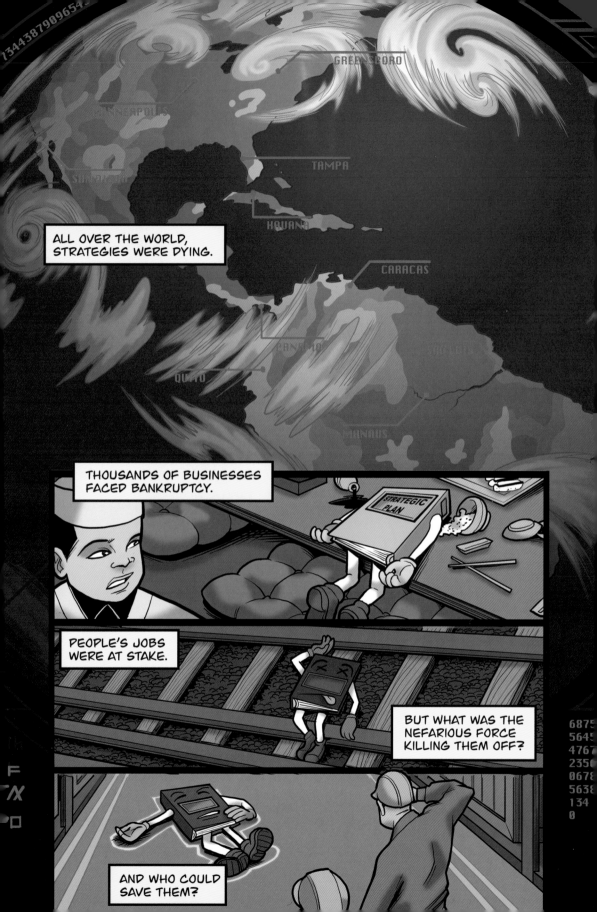

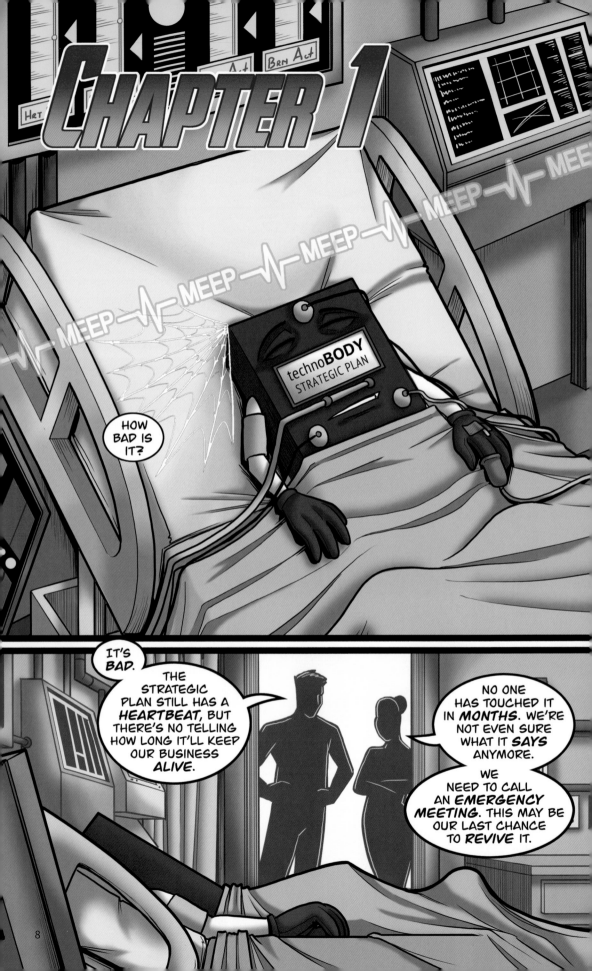

11

15

LATER, AT THE **STRATEGIC THINKING INSTITUTE** . . .

WELCOME BACK, STRATEGYMAN! WELL DONE.

I'M JUST DOING THE LATEST RESEARCH FOR OUR CURRENT CASE . . .

A survey of 400 managers found that only 44.3% of organizations have a universal definition of strategy, and less than half (46%) have a common language for strategy.[1]

This inconsistent understanding leads to confusion, inefficiency, and bad strategy. In fact, research published in the *Harvard Business Review* showed that 67% of managers surveyed believe that their companies are bad at developing strategy.[2]

When you couple these facts with research showing that the number one cause of business failure, more than 80% of the time, is bad strategy, it makes for a dangerous combination.[3]

RICH, THAT REMINDS ME OF SOME OF OUR BIGGEST CASES OF MISTAKEN STRATEGY IDENTITY.

"STRATEGIES" AT COMPANIES ACROSS INDUSTRIES, INCLUDING FORTUNE 500 COMPANIES

—Become more profitable.
—Grow our audience.
—Become number one in the market.
—Execute integration, and capture synergies.
—Strengthen core business, and reduce costs.
—Find people who were customers and didn't come back.

How to Defeat
Jargon Goblin and Ignormous

1. Stop mixing words.
Since "strategy" is an abstract term, it's challenging enough to define it without combining it with other words to make it that much more confusing. Many companies use terms such as "strategic goals" and "strategic objectives." Why? Goals and objectives are different than strategies, so cramming the words together into one term only serves to muddy the waters. To refresh, the goal is generally what you are trying to achieve (e.g., increase sales). The objective is specifically what you are trying to achieve (e.g., increase sales by 15% in the east region by Q4). The strategy is how you will achieve the goal/objective (e.g., develop a real-time service model to support top-tier product users). Keep your plan simple by using the right word, and *only* the word, that you mean.

2. Stop making things up.
Creativity is great. However, when it comes to setting strategic direction, creating new terms is inefficient and potentially harmful. Words such as "goal," "objective," "strategy," and "tactic" all have concrete definitions that originated in the military arena thousands of years ago. Terms like "strategic imperatives" or "business drivers" are not foundational planning terms. And because they are not foundational concepts, they can be interpreted in lots of different ways. This can lead to miscommunication, misunderstanding, and misdirection. When planning, use real words, not made-up ones.

3. Stop pretending.
If a leader in your company passes down a strategy that isn't really a strategy, stop pretending it is. Correct it! In the examples listed earlier, many of the so-called strategies are actually goals or operating initiatives. Anyone working under similar "strategies" should choose the right forum and appropriate time to talk to leadership about how to modify their statement to more accurately reflect a strategy.

31

THINKTION: Transforming thinking into action

The mission statement helps frame the business strategy. As the mission statement addresses the scope of business, customer targets, and competitive arena, it naturally shapes the business strategy.

...n statement helps frame the business strategy. As the mission statement addresses the scope of business, customer targets, and competitive arena, it naturally shapes the business strategy.

It also forces decisions of what not to do, one of the key characteristics of strategic thinking. When a company chooses what not to do and who not to target as customers, the business focus emerges.

THE NOTED MILITARY HISTORIAN B. H. LIDDELL HART POINTED TO THE IMPORTANCE OF FOCUS WHEN HE SAID,

"THE PRINCIPLES OF WAR CAN BE CONDENSED INTO ONE WORD: CONCENTRATION."[2]

Examples of mission statements include the following:

FACEBOOK

To give people the power to share and make the world more open and connected.

MOLESKIN NOTEBOOKS

Offering people a platform to express themselves and their creativity.

LEGO

Inspire and develop the builders of tomorrow.

and the longer version:

Our ultimate purpose is to inspire and develop children to think creatively, reason systematically, and release their potential to shape their own future—experiencing the endless human possibility.

Mission serves as the current purpose.

Actions | Reply | Reply All | Forward | Delete | Tools

COMPOSE

Inbox (4)
Sent
Drafts
Spam
Trash

StrategyMan
Purposeider

Re: Top Tips for Mission, Vision, and Value Statements

2. Vision is the future purpose, providing a mental picture of the aspirational existence an organization is working toward. The vision statement provides two things: strategic guidance and motivational focus.

MISSION = CURRENT

VISION = FUTURE

YES, RICH, THE STRATEGIC THINKING THAT GOES INTO CREATING THE VISION —THE *FUTURE PURPOSE*—ENSURES IT REPRESENTS THE BEST USE OF THE ORGANIZATION'S RESOURCES IN REACHING ITS GOALS.

THE VISION SERVES TO ALIGN INDIVIDUALS FROM DIFFERENT FUNCTIONAL AREAS AND GEOGRAPHIC LOCATIONS TO MOVE TOWARD THE SAME FUTURE PURPOSE. THIS ALLOWS THEM TO USE THEIR CREATIVITY AND TALENTS TO GET FROM "HERE" TO "THERE." IT GUIDES THEIR ACTIONS BY SHOWING THE DESIRED LONG-TERM FUTURE AND THE BENEFITS OF REALIZING THAT FUTURE.

I'M NOTICING THERE IS SOMETIMES CONFUSION BETWEEN THE GOAL AND THE VISION, BECAUSE BOTH ARE ASPIRATIONS. A KEY DISTINCTION BETWEEN THE TWO TERMS IS THE ACTUAL ATTAINMENT. GOALS ARE MEANT TO BE ACHIEVED ON A REGULAR BASIS AND THEN REPLACED WITH NEW GOALS THAT ADVANCE THE BUSINESS. A VISION IS MEANT TO CREATE ENDURING AMBITION OVER LONGER PERIODS OF TIME.

VISION = ENDURING AMBITION

GOALS = REGULAR ACHIEVEMENT AND RE-CREATION

FOR EXAMPLE, PART OF THE LEGO COMPANY'S VISION IS "INVENTING THE FUTURE OF PLAY. WE WANT TO PIONEER NEW WAYS OF PLAYING..."

AS YOU CAN SEE, "INVENTING THE FUTURE OF PLAY" IS A CONTINUOUS, LONG-TERM PURSUIT. IT PROVIDES A COMPELLING FOUNDATION FOR THE AMBITIOUS JOURNEY TO THEIR ASPIRATIONAL DESTINATION.

STRATEGYMAN

35

Re: Top Tips for Mission, Vision, and Value Statements

3. The daily manifestation of purpose comes in the form of values. Values are the principles that guide the thoughts and actions of a company's personnel. Too often, values are chosen based on the highest ideals people imagine rather than what's true to the organization.

VALUES SHOULD BE THOUGHTFULLY SELECTED BY LEADERS TO REINFORCE THE TRAITS THEY BELIEVE DIFFERENTIATE THEM FROM OTHERS AND WILL FUEL SUCCESS.

VALUES ARE *NOT* SHORT-TERM IDENTITIES; THEY REPRESENT THE LONG-TERM BEHAVIORS THAT BECOME *INGRAINED* IN THE GROUP'S DNA.

FOR INSTANCE, *DISNEY* HAS THE FOLLOWING VALUES: INNOVATION, QUALITY, COMMUNITY, STORYTELLING, OPTIMISM, AND DECENCY.

WHEN YOU VISIT A DISNEY PROPERTY, IT'S FAIR TO SAY THAT EACH OF THESE VALUES IS ON DISPLAY. *STORYTELLING* IS AT THE HEART OF DISNEY, AND THE ENTERTAINMENT THEY PRODUCE FOSTERS THE VALUE OF *COMMUNITY*.

THE STORIES AND CHARACTERS BRING AN AIR OF *OPTIMISM*, GIVING RISE TO HOPE AND ASPIRATION. THE *QUALITY* OF DISNEY'S PRODUCTS AND SERVICES IS WORLD-RENOWNED.

AT HIS COMMENCEMENT SPEECH TO THE HARVARD SCHOOL OF DESIGN, ACCLAIMED DESIGNER JAMES ROUSE SAID, "DISNEYLAND... TOOK AN AREA OF ACTIVITY—THE AMUSEMENT PARK—AND LIFTED IT TO A STANDARD SO HIGH IN ITS PERFORMANCE, IN ITS RESPECT FOR PEOPLE, IN ITS FUNCTIONING FOR PEOPLE, THAT IT REALLY BECAME A BRAND NEW THING."[3]

WHILE MANY COMPANIES LIST INNOVATION AS A VALUE, DISNEY HAS ALWAYS LIVED IT. WHEN HIS BOARD OF DIRECTORS PUSHED BACK ON THE DISNEYLAND CONCEPT, WALT TOOK AN EMOTIONAL STAND: "THERE'S NOTHING LIKE IT IN THE WORLD. I KNOW, BECAUSE I'VE LOOKED. THAT'S WHY IT CAN BE GREAT: BECAUSE IT WILL BE UNIQUE. A NEW CONCEPT IN ENTERTAINMENT."[4] INDEED, DISNEY CONTINUES TO INNOVATE TODAY. DISNEY DEMONSTRATES THE POWER OF VALUES WHEN THEY ARE DIFFERENTIATING AND TRUE.

THE PURPOSE TRIDENT

MISSION

In developing your mission statement, consider the following five questions:

1. What function is performed?
2. How is the function performed?
3. For whom is the function performed?
4. Why is the function performed?
5. What tone will convey the company's uniqueness?

VISION

In developing your vision statement, see if it meets the following five criteria:

1. Does it paint a picture of the desired future?
2. Will it create a burning ambition?
3. Is it distinct from long-term goals?
4. Does it allow for creativity and flexibility?
5. Can people imagine the realistic pursuit of it?

VALUES

In developing your values, consider the following criteria:

1. Do they reflect what we truly believe?
2. Are they different from others in our space?
3. Are we committed to really living these each day?
4. Is the group of values concise enough to be memorable?
5. Will these be the enduring traits that lead us to our vision?

TIME TWISTER AND FIRE DRILLER ARE TWO OF BUSINESSES' MOST DANGEROUS VILLAINS.

THEY ARE POLAR OPPOSITES: TIME TWISTER QUIETLY STEALS YOUR TIME WHILE FIRE DRILLER USES THE ADRENALINE RUSH OF PUTTING OUT FIRES TO CREATE A SIZZLING COMMOTION.

IN BOTH CASES, YOUR TIME IS HIJACKED BY PEOPLE, EVENTS, OR ISSUES. IT'S UP TO YOU TO TAKE IT BACK.

I DEAL WITH THESE TWO A LOT. A STUDY RICH CONDUCTED OF MORE THAN 500 MANAGERS AT 25 COMPANIES SHOWED THAT THE NUMBER ONE STRATEGY CHALLENGE IS TIME.[1]

THE MOST COMMON BELIEF I'VE HEARD IS THAT THERE ISN'T TIME IN BUSY SCHEDULES TO STOP AND THINK ABOUT STRATEGY. THERE ARE TOO MANY ITEMS ON THE TO-DO LIST TO DEVOTE REGULAR PERIODS OF TIME TO THINKING STRATEGICALLY, WHETHER IT BE INDIVIDUALLY OR IN GROUPS.

MANY MANAGERS ALSO NOTE THAT TIME SPENT THINKING STRATEGICALLY ISN'T ONE OF THE METRICS BY WHICH THEIR PERFORMANCE IS MEASURED. SOME PROFESSIONALS THINK THEIR CULTURE DOESN'T SUPPORT TAKING TIME OUT TO THINK OR DOESN'T HAVE A FRAMEWORK OR PROCESS FOR PRODUCTIVE THINKING AND PLANNING.

"Just as you would not permit a fellow employee to steal a piece of office equipment, you shouldn't let anyone walk away with the time of his fellow managers."
—Former Intel CEO Andy Grove[2]

Examples of internal fires include:

- Senior leaders demanding manual lists or reports that require time, labor, and energy to put together, versus those that can be automatically generated.
- Flavor-of-the-month initiatives that aren't directly related to people's strategic plans.
- Attendance on conference calls that have no direct business value for the participant.

Examples of external fires include:

- The same customer continually asking for activities to be performed in a much shorter time frame than normal.
- Requests for proposals that don't match up with your business acquisition criteria.
- People outside the organization seeking teleconferences or meetings to discuss partnerships or alliances without first providing sufficient business rationale.

I WISH WE COULD PREVENT THESE KINDS OF CALLS. THIS PLACE IS A MESS.

WELL, JUST AS FIRE REQUIRES OXYGEN TO BURN, FIRE DRILLS REQUIRE ATTENTION TO FAN THEIR FLAMES. FIRE DRILLS CAN BECOME A HABIT AND CONSUME A DISPROPORTIONATE AMOUNT OF RESOURCES.

A HABIT IS DEFINED AS, "A BEHAVIOR PATTERN ACQUIRED BY FREQUENT REPETITION; AN ACQUIRED MODE OF BEHAVIOR THAT HAS BECOME NEARLY OR COMPLETELY INVOLUNTARY."[7]

DEPENDING ON THE BEHAVIOR, THE HABIT CAN BE POSITIVE, LIKE EXERCISING EACH MORNING, OR NEGATIVE, SUCH AS UNCONTROLLED GAMBLING.

THE GOAL IS TO FOSTER POSITIVE HABITS AND TRANSFORM NEGATIVE HABITS INTO POSITIVE ONES. AS ANYONE WHO HAS TRIED TO BREAK A BAD HABIT KNOWS, IT'S MUCH EASIER SAID THAN DONE.

Researchers at the Massachusetts Institute of Technology have shed light on the science behind habits.

A habit consists of the following three components:

1. Cue (trigger)
2. Routine (behavior)
3. Reward (result)[8]

This neurological loop is at the core of our habits, both good and bad. The cue for a positive habit like exercising in the morning might be your dog waking you up at six a.m. with a lick on the hand. The routine would be jogging along the lake, and the reward is an ice-cold chocolate protein shake.

The cue for a detrimental habit, like uncontrolled gambling, might be boredom. The routine would be going to a casino and playing poker, and the reward is the excitement (or lack of boredom) that comes from winning or from the near misses of almost winning.

ALL HABITS FOLLOW THIS PATH OF CUE, ROUTINE, AND REWARD.

WE CAN USE THIS HABIT MODEL TO IMPROVE OUR APPROACH TO STRATEGY BY CREATING GOOD HABITS AND ELIMINATING NEGATIVE ONES SUCH AS FIRE DRILLS.

IF YOUR TEAM IS SEDUCED BY FIREFIGHTING, THEN CONSIDER ADOPTING THE FOLLOWING TECHNIQUE WHEN THE FIRE DRILL ALARM IS SOUNDED.

BBBRRRRIIIIINNNNNGG

THE FIRE DRILL IS WHEN PEOPLE STOP PURPOSEFUL WORK GUIDED BY THEIR STRATEGIC PLAN AND RUSH TO TAKE CARE OF SOMETHING THAT JUST POPPED UP.

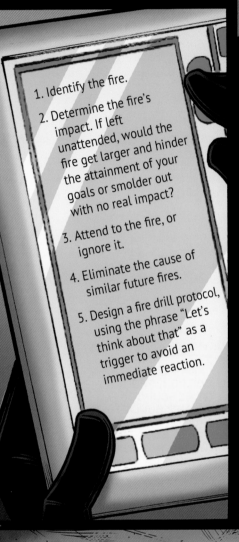

1. Identify the fire.

2. Determine the fire's impact. If left unattended, would the fire get larger and hinder the attainment of your goals or smolder out with no real impact?

3. Attend to the fire, or ignore it.

4. Eliminate the cause of similar future fires.

5. Design a fire drill protocol, using the phrase "Let's think about that" as a trigger to avoid an immediate reaction.

IF THE URGENT ISSUE IS ALSO IMPORTANT, THEN NATURALLY IT SHOULD BE TAKEN CARE OF. UNFORTUNATELY, MANY FIRES ARE URGENT BUT UNIMPORTANT. YET THEY STILL GET LOTS OF ATTENTION, WHICH WASTES VALUABLE TIME, PEOPLE, AND BUDGET.

The key to eliminating a bad habit is to replace the routine, or behavior, with a more positive or productive one. By keeping the same cue and same reward, this shift in routine can transform the bad habit into a good one.

In the fire drill example, it's to be expected that fires will continue to pop up during the course of business, even if some can be prevented by understanding the root causes in their systems. When the cue or fire triggers the habit, however, we need to replace the current routine—a flurry of unplanned activity—with a new one.

A phrase as simple as "Let's think about that" can initiate the new routine. This phrase reminds people not to just react to the fire but to consider it relative to the other planned initiatives currently at stake.

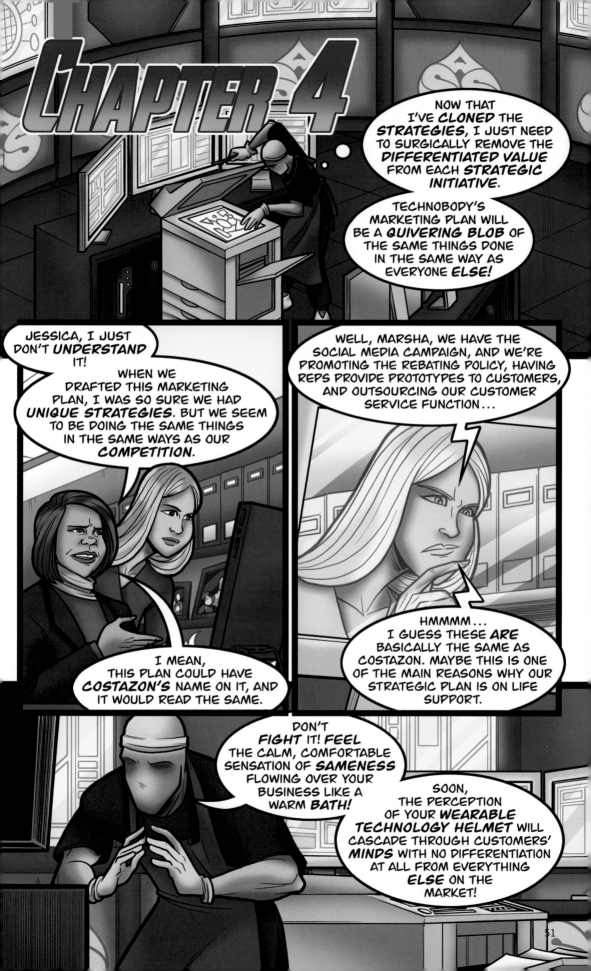

53

THINKTION:
Transforming Thinking /Action

TCH-TCHEEEEEEEE

THE ENTERTAINMENT INDUSTRY PROVIDES A GOOD EXAMPLE OF THE FINANCIAL POWER OF DIFFERENTIATION. IF YOU HAVE KIDS, NIECES, NEPHEWS, OR GRANDCHILDREN, THERE'S A GOOD CHANCE YOU'VE SEEN ONE OR MORE OF THE FOLLOWING FILMS: TOY STORY (1, 2, 3), MONSTERS (INC., UNIVERSITY), A BUG'S LIFE, FINDING NEMO, THE INCREDIBLES, CARS (1, 2, 3), RATATOUILLE, WALL-E, UP, BRAVE, INSIDE OUT, AND THE GOOD DINOSAUR.

TOGETHER, THESE DAZZLING FILMS HAVE GARNERED DOZENS OF ACADEMY AWARDS AND HAVE RUNG UP SALES OF MORE THAN $5 BILLION. WHAT'S MORE AMAZING IS THEY HAVE ALL BEEN CREATED BY ONE COMPANY: PIXAR.

BAMF
BAMF
BAMF
BAMF

ED CATMULL, COFOUNDER AND NOW PRESIDENT OF PIXAR AND DISNEY ANIMATION STUDIOS, ATTRIBUTES THEIR SUCCESS TO DIFFERENTIATION: "WE AS EXECUTIVES HAVE TO RESIST OUR NATURAL TENDENCY TO AVOID OR MINIMIZE RISKS, WHICH OF COURSE IS MUCH EASIER SAID THAN DONE. IN THE MOVIE BUSINESS, THIS INSTINCT LEADS EXECUTIVES TO CHOOSE TO COPY SUCCESSES RATHER THAN TRY TO CREATE SOMETHING BRAND NEW.

THAT'S WHY YOU SEE SO MANY MOVIES THAT ARE SO MUCH ALIKE. IT ALSO EXPLAINS WHY A LOT OF FILMS AREN'T VERY GOOD. IF YOU WANT TO BE ORIGINAL, YOU HAVE TO ACCEPT THE UNCERTAINTY, EVEN WHEN IT'S UNCOMFORTABLE, AND HAVE THE CAPABILITY TO RECOVER WHEN YOUR ORGANIZATION TAKES A BIG RISK AND FAILS."[2]

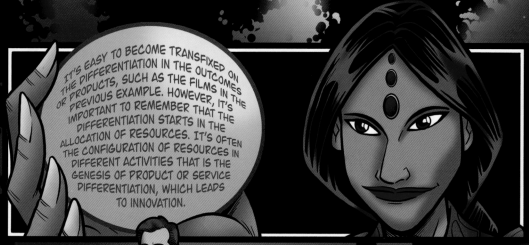

IT'S EASY TO BECOME TRANSFIXED ON THE DIFFERENTIATION IN THE OUTCOMES OR PRODUCTS, SUCH AS THE FILMS IN THE PREVIOUS EXAMPLE. HOWEVER, IT'S IMPORTANT TO REMEMBER THAT THE DIFFERENTIATION STARTS IN THE ALLOCATION OF RESOURCES. IT'S OFTEN THE CONFIGURATION OF RESOURCES IN DIFFERENT ACTIVITIES THAT IS THE GENESIS OF PRODUCT OR SERVICE DIFFERENTIATION, WHICH LEADS TO INNOVATION.

RESEARCH SHOWS THAT COMPANIES TEND TO ALLOCATE 90% OR MORE OF THEIR RESOURCES TO THE SAME PLACES YEAR IN AND YEAR OUT.[3] BUT, DURING THE 15-YEAR STUDY, THE FIRMS THAT REALLOCATED THE MOST RESOURCES— MORE THAN 50% OF CAPITAL ON AVERAGE ACROSS DIVISIONS—ACHIEVED 30% HIGHER SHAREHOLDER RETURNS THAN THOSE FIRMS THAT REALLOCATED LEAST.[4] ALLOWING A STATUS QUO MINDSET TO LIMIT YOUR REALLOCATION OF RESOURCES IS ONE OF THE GREATEST THREATS TO YOUR COMPANY'S PROFITABLE GROWTH.

TAKE A MOMENT AND ANSWER THESE 10 QUESTIONS RELATED TO DIFFERENTIATION:

1. What activities of ours are truly different from the competition?
2. What similar activities do we perform differently from the competition?
3. How is our business model different from the competition?
4. What resources do we have that are different from the competition?
5. How do our core competencies differ from those of our competitors?
6. How do customers describe the differences between the competition and us?
7. How does our culture differ from our closest competitor?
8. Are there any real differences between our people and our competitors' people?
9. How does our professional development differ from that of competitors?
10. What is the primary differentiated value our offering provides to customers?

THE KEY WEAPON FOR DEFEATING THE SAME IS THE *TRADE-OFF ZONE.*

GOOD STRATEGY DEMANDS DIFFERENTIATION, WHICH MEANS TRADE-OFFS: CHOOSING ONE PATH AND NOT THE OTHER.

COMPANIES TRYING TO BE ALL THINGS TO ALL PEOPLE ARE THE EASIEST TO BEAT.

THE MARK OF A *GREAT* COMPANY IS THAT THEIR DIFFERENTIATION CREATES TRADE-OFFS THAT COMPETITORS CANNOT OR WILL NOT MEET.

WEAPON:
TRADE-OFF
ZONE

A TOOL THAT CAN BE USED TO HELP GAUGE YOUR DIFFERENTIATION RELATIVE TO THE COMPETITION IS THE *TRADE-OFF ZONE.*

IT'S A VISUAL REPRESENTATION OF THE DIFFERENTIATION, OR LACK THEREOF, BEING MADE IN A MARKET.

THE TOOL IDENTIFIES COMMON TRADE-OFF FACTORS THAT FIGURE PROMINENTLY IN THE CUSTOMER'S VALUE EQUATION.

FIVE COMMON BENEFIT FACTORS ARE: 1) QUALITY, 2) CONVENIENCE, 3) COST, 4) SERVICE, AND 5) SELECTION.

COMPETITORS ARE PLOTTED IN THE LOW, MEDIUM, OR HIGH ZONE FOR EACH FACTOR BASED ON THEIR PERFORMANCE DELIVERING THAT BENEFIT.

DEPENDING ON THE BUSINESS, THESE FACTORS CAN BE USED OR OTHERS CAN BE SUBSTITUTED IF THEY ARE MORE RELEVANT TO THAT SPECIFIC MARKET.

TO CONSTRUCT A TRADE-OFF ZONE FOR YOUR BUSINESS, FIRST SELECT THE SPECIFIC TYPE OF CUSTOMER THAT THE OFFER TARGETS.

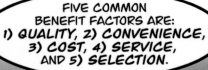

IN SOME CASES, THE ROOT OF POOR STRATEGY IS TRYING TO BE ALL THINGS TO ALL CUSTOMERS. IF SOME POTENTIAL CUSTOMERS ARE NOT HAPPY WITH HOW YOU CHOOSE TO BRING VALUE TO THE MARKET, IT'S A SIGN THAT TRADE-OFFS HAVE BEEN MADE.

THE POINT IS THAT EFFECTIVE STRATEGY IS GOING TO UPSET SOME POTENTIAL INTERNAL OR EXTERNAL CUSTOMERS. LEARN TO LIVE WITH IT. JUST AS A REAL LEADER ISN'T GOING TO PLEASE ALL POTENTIAL FOLLOWERS, A REAL STRATEGY ISN'T GOING TO PLEASE ALL POTENTIAL CUSTOMERS.

ONCE THAT'S DONE, A MANAGER CAN RATE THEIR OFFERING FOR EACH OF THE TRADE-OFF FACTORS AS LOW, MEDIUM, OR HIGH, AS SEEN BY THE TARGETED CUSTOMER.

HIGH
MED
LOW

#2

COMPETITIVE OFFERINGS ARE THEN PLOTTED, CREATING TRADE-OFF PROFILES, TO DETERMINE WHERE DIFFERENTIATION EXISTS WITHIN THE TRADE-OFF ZONE.

VS.

#3

IF YOUR TRADE-OFF PROFILE MIRRORS THE COMPETITION, WORK NEEDS TO BE DONE TO DETERMINE THE TRADE-OFF FACTORS, TARGETED CUSTOMERS' VALUE, AND HOW TO CREATE POSITIVE DIFFERENTIATION AROUND THEM.

#4

HERE IS AN EXAMPLE OF THE TRADE-OFF ZONE FOR TECHNOBODY AND COSTAZON.

USING THE TRADE-OFF ZONE, IT BECOMES APPARENT WHICH BENEFIT FACTORS EACH COMPANY IS USING TO STEER CUSTOMERS TO THEIR OFFERING.

CUSTOMERS WITH A GREATER DEMAND FOR QUALITY AND SERVICE WOULD BE MORE LIKELY TO CHOOSE TECHNOBODY, WHILE CUSTOMERS MORE INTERESTED IN COST SAVINGS, SELECTION, AND EASE OF USE WOULD PREFER COSTAZON.

Trade-Off Zone

	Low	Medium	High
Price			
Quality			
Service			
Selection			
Ease of Use			

Costazon: ●——● TechnoBody: ○----○

THE TRADE-OFF PROFILE SHOULD SHOW POINTS OF DIFFERENCE AMONG THE BENEFIT FACTORS.

IF YOU ARE BRINGING DIFFERENTIATED VALUE TO CUSTOMERS, THIS WILL BE REFLECTED IN DIFFERENCES IN THE TRADE-OFF ZONE.

IF YOUR OFFERING IS AT PARITY, YOU'LL SEE COMPETITIVE CONVERGENCE OR A MIRRORING OF TRADE-OFF PROFILES WITH YOUR COMPETITION.

GREAT! THANKS, EVERYONE! LUKE, LET'S BRING THIS BACK TO THE TEAM.

MEEP MEEP

63

69

71

Solve Their Challenge!

IF WE DEFINE A CHALLENGE AS DIFFICULTY OR DISSATISFACTION WITH AN ACTIVITY, TASK, OR THE STATUS QUO THAT IS STIMULATING TO SOMEONE ENGAGED IN IT BECAUSE THE SOLUTION LEADS TO PROGRESS...THEN PROGRESS MANIFESTS ITSELF IN THE NEW VALUE PRODUCED BY HELPING THOSE YOU SERVE SOLVE THEIR PROBLEMS.

IF YOU WANT TO MOVE OUT OF A REACTIVE MODE, YOU MUST HELP CUSTOMERS SOLVE THEIR CURRENT CHALLENGES.

EXACTLY! ENTREPRENEUR JAMES DYSON SPENT DECADES WORKING ON A VACUUM TECHNOLOGY TO HELP PEOPLE WITH THE VERY COMMON CHALLENGE OF CLEANING.

HE SAID, "I LIKE FRUSTRATION. I LIKE SEEING THINGS IN EVERYDAY LIFE THAT DON'T WORK VERY WELL AND TRY TO MAKE THEM BETTER."[4]

ONE EFFECTIVE WAY OF INNOVATING, OR CREATING NEW VALUE, IS TO LOOK AT YOUR MARKET, CUSTOMERS, COMPETITORS, AND YOUR OWN COMPANY, AND ASK, "WHAT ARE THE PRIMARY CHALLENGES PEOPLE FACE?"

CONSIDER FUNCTIONAL ACTIVITIES, TASKS, PROCESSES, INTERNAL AND EXTERNAL ASPECTS. IF YOU FEEL YOUR GROUP IS TOO CAUGHT UP IN THE FEATURE/BENEFIT BATTLE WITH COMPETITORS, COME BACK TO THE KEY CHALLENGES OR PROBLEMS AND HOW TO SOLVE THEM IN WAYS THAT INTRODUCE NEW VALUE.

BEFORE REVOLUTIONIZING THE VACUUM WITH HIS CYCLONE TECHNOLOGY AND SEE-THROUGH, BAGLESS CANISTER, DYSON SOLVED A PROBLEM COMMON TO MANY OF HIS BRITISH NEIGHBORS WHO WORKED IN THEIR YARDS:

WHEELBARROWS GETTING THEIR TIRES STUCK IN THE MUD. INSTEAD OF A "WHEEL" BARROW, HE INTRODUCED THE BALLBARROW, WHICH USED A BALL INSTEAD TO SOLVE THE PROBLEM OF THE WHEELS GETTING STUCK.

Innovate by Solving Their Challenge: What two to three significant challenges do my customers face that we should spend time to try and solve?

Jump the Domain!

WHEN A TV SHOW JUMPS THE SHARK, IT'S BAD NEWS. BUT JUMPING THE DOMAIN IS GOOD NEWS.

IT CAN MEAN INNOVATION. WE TEND TO OPERATE IN FAIRLY FINITE DOMAINS OF OUR INDUSTRY, MARKET, AND PRODUCT OR SERVICE CATEGORIES.

THINKING ALONG THESE LINES ON A REGULAR BASIS CREATES MENTAL TRACKS, WHICH STREAMLINE TYPICAL BUSINESS ACTIVITIES. HOWEVER, WHEN IT COMES TO THINKING IN DIFFERENT WAYS, THESE TRACKS CAN BECOME RUTS.

IN THE INNOVATIVE THINKING WORKSHOPS I LEAD, WE GO THROUGH AN EXERCISE I CREATED CALLED DOMAIN JUMPING.

IT'S AN EXCELLENT TECHNIQUE TO EXTRACT PEOPLE FROM THEIR MENTAL RUTS AND GIVE THEM NEW PERSPECTIVES IN WHICH TO VIEW THEIR BUSINESS.

ONE EXAMPLE OF DOMAIN JUMPING COMES FROM A COMPANY CALLED SHARKLET TECHNOLOGIES. THE COMPANY EVOLVED FROM THE DOMAIN JUMPING OF TONY BRENNAN.

TASKED WITH FINDING A MORE EFFECTIVE MEANS OF REDUCING THE AMOUNT OF BARNACLES ON NAVY SHIPS, HE DISCOVERED THE COMPOSITION OF SHARK'S SKIN AS A CARPET-LIKE MATERIAL OF TINY TEETH. THESE SMALL, BUMPY SCALES ON THE SHARK PREVENT ALGAE AND BARNACLES FROM GAINING A HOLD ON IT.

AFTER HE CREATED THE SHIP APPLICATION, THE COMPANY MOVED TO SHARKSKIN-INSPIRED, TEXTURED-FILM PRODUCTS THAT PREVENT BACTERIAL ADHESION.

SOME OF THESE PRODUCTS HAVE BEEN HELPFUL IN PLACES SUCH AS HOSPITALS, WHERE LIGHT SWITCHES, HANDLES, AND COUNTERS CAN HOUSE BACTERIA, WHICH LEADS TO A GREATER INCIDENCE OF INFECTIONS. ALL POSSIBLE BECAUSE SOMEONE JUMPED THEIR DOMAIN.

Innovate by Jumping the Domain: Identify a challenge your company faces, and jump to another domain by asking: "How would Disney, a detective, or an Indy pit crew approach this?"

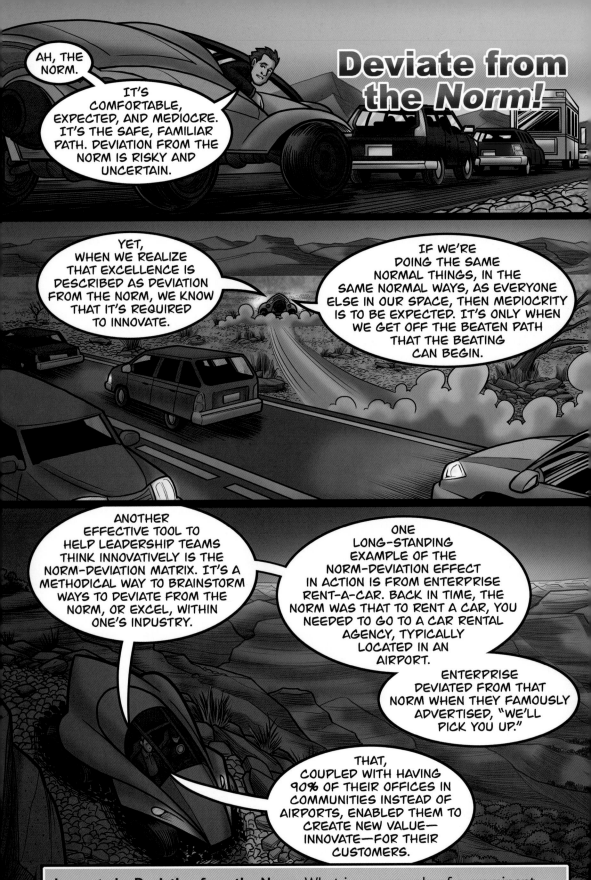

Innovate by Deviating from the Norm: What is an example of a prominent industry norm in our space and how might we deviate from it?

THE VALUE MINING MATRIX CONSIDERS CUSTOMERS AND THE JOBS THEY NEED FULFILLED.

AS YOU'LL RECALL, THESE ARE TWO OF THE PRIMARY ELEMENTS OF THE VALUE PROPOSITION WE'VE ALREADY LOOKED AT. IN THIS EXERCISE, CUSTOMERS ARE THOUGHT OF AS CURRENT, THOSE YOU'RE ACTIVELY MARKETING TO, SELLING TO, SERVING, OR SUPPORTING TODAY.

VALUE MINING MATRIX

OR, CUSTOMERS ARE THOUGHT OF AS POTENTIAL, MEANING GROUPS OR TYPES OF CUSTOMERS YOU'RE NOT ACTIVELY MARKETING TO, SELLING TO, SERVING, OR SUPPORTING TODAY.

THESE POTENTIAL CUSTOMERS MAY BE INFLUENCERS, DECISION MAKERS, OR END USERS THAT FIND VALUE IN WHAT YOU'RE ABLE TO PROVIDE.

THE JOB AXIS VIEWS CUSTOMER JOBS THAT NEED TO BE FULFILLED AS EITHER EXISTING TODAY—CURRENT NEEDS—OR EMERGING.

EMERGING JOBS WOULD CONSIST OF FUTURE NEEDS THAT CUSTOMERS WOULD FIND VALUE IN HAVING FULFILLED BY YOUR ORGANIZATION.

THE JOBS TO BE DONE MAY NOT BE IDENTIFIED, TALKED ABOUT, OR EVEN NOTICED BY YOUR CUSTOMERS BUT OFTEN MANIFEST THEMSELVES AS THE PROBLEMS, PAINS, OR CHALLENGES THEY FACE.

WHILE PROGRAMS SUCH AS THE "VOICE OF THE CUSTOMER" ARE HELPFUL IN GAINING A DEEPER UNDERSTANDING OF CUSTOMERS' REACTIONS TO CURRENT OFFERINGS, THEY MAY NOT ELICIT DEEPER INSIGHTS ABOUT THEIR REAL NEEDS.

THESE DEEPER INSIGHTS CAN OFTEN BE GLEANED BY SIMPLY OBSERVING YOUR CUSTOMERS IN THEIR DAY-TO-DAY ACTIVITIES AND NOTING THE ISSUES, PROBLEMS, AND CHALLENGES THAT ARISE.

CREATING A LIST OF THEIR "JOBS TO BE DONE" IS AN EFFECTIVE WAY TO BEGIN THE VALUE MINING PROCESS.

VALUE MINING MATRIX

CVS HEALTH'S MINUTECLINIC
CURRENT CUSTOMER BASE HAD A NEED
FOR AN EXISTING SERVICE, WHICH
WAS QUICK, CONVENIENT CARE FOR
NON-EMERGENCY MEDICAL CONDITIONS.
THIS JOB WAS NOT BEING FULFILLED
ADEQUATELY BY PHYSICIAN VISITS,
WHICH ARE OFTEN NOT CONVENIENT
OR EFFICIENT ENOUGH FOR PATIENTS.

LEGO WAS ABLE TO TAP INTO THE EXISTING
NEED FOR AN ENTERTAINING TOY THAT
HELPS TO PROMOTE CHILDREN'S SPATIAL
SKILLS. THE COMPANY CHOSE TO FOCUS
ON YOUNG GIRLS, WHO HAD BEEN LESS
ENGAGED WITH THE BRAND THAN BOYS.

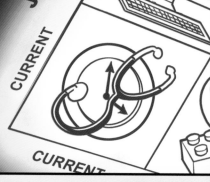

BY OFFERING THE *MINUTECLINICS* IN
THEIR STORE LOCATIONS, CVS HEALTH
WAS ABLE TO DRIVE PROFITABLE GROWTH
BY SERVING CURRENT CUSTOMERS WITH
AN EXISTING JOB TO BE DONE (QUICK,
CONVENIENT MEDICAL CARE).

THE *LEGO FRIENDS* SERIES PROVIDES
YOUNG GIRLS WITH THE OPPORTUNITY TO
BUILD, SOCIALIZE, AND CREATE WITH
FEMALE CHARACTERS IN SETTINGS SUCH
AS HORSE STABLES AND CAMPGROUNDS.

THE EMERGING JOB IN THIS CASE WAS TO FIND NEW TELEVISION PROGRAMS THAT CAN BE CONSUMED IN A BINGE FORMAT INSTEAD OF WAITING A WEEK TO WATCH THE NEXT EPISODE.

THE CONVENIENCE OF BEING ABLE TO STREAM THE ORIGINAL CONTENT ON DIFFERENT DEVICES PROVIDES CURRENT CUSTOMERS OF NETFLIX WITH BOTH NEW CONTENT AND NEW ACCESS TO ENTERTAINMENT.

BY PROVIDING ON-DEMAND COMPUTER SERVICES VIA THE CLOUD TO OTHER BUSINESSES RANGING FROM NETFLIX TO NASA, *AMAZON'S* CLOUD SERVICE INITIALLY SERVED NEW CUSTOMERS FOR AMAZON THAT HAD A NEW JOB TO GET DONE.

TOO OFTEN, IDEAS FOR GROWTH ARE SEEN FROM A PRODUCT POINT OF VIEW, INSTEAD OF A NEED OR JOB-TO-BE-FULFILLED PERSPECTIVE.

THE VALUE MINING MATRIX REFOCUSES YOUR TEAM ON THE FOUNDATIONAL CORE OF VALUE: CUSTOMERS AND NEEDS, PROVIDING YOU WITH A WELLSPRING OF INNOVATION.

HI CARL.

OH, HEY, MARK.

LINDA, DO *YOU* HEAR THAT NOISE?

UM... NO.

IT SEEMS THERE'S A DELAY WITH THE NEW CRM SYSTEM, AND IT WON'T BE READY FOR ANOTHER SIX WEEKS.

ACTUALLY, THAT'S RIGHT ON SCHEDULE, ACCORDING TO *SHAUN'S* LAST UPDATE.

WELL, MARSHA THINKS IT'S BEHIND SCHEDULE, AND SHE'S WAITING FOR IT TO UPDATE HER MARKETING PLAN.

THERE SEEMS TO BE A LOT OF MISCOMMUNICATION GOING ON.

LET'S USE OUR MEETING TOMORROW TO GET PEOPLE ON THE SAME PAGE.

AND *I'LL* BE SURE IT GOES NOWHERE FAST.

THINKTION:
TRANSFORMING THINKING INTO ACTION

HERE ARE TWO WAYS TO SPAN THE SILOS IN YOUR ORGANIZATION AND HAVE MORE EFFECTIVE MEETINGS:

1. Create an insight network

An insight is when you're able to combine two or more pieces of information or data into a new solution, new offering, or new approach to creating value.

A study of more than 5,000 executives showed that the most important innovation trait for managers in high-performing organizations is the ability to come up with insights.[6]

Unfortunately, only 35% of managers believe their strategies are built on unique insights.[7] This is a big reason that so many products and services devolve into "me-too" offerings with no differentiation and are left to battle it out on price.

AN INSIGHT NETWORK CAN ENSURE YOU'RE CONTINUALLY IN TUNE WITH IDEAS FROM ALL OVER YOUR ORGANIZATION.

TO BUILD AN INSIGHT NETWORK, MAP OUT THE DIFFERENT PLAYERS IN THE ORGANIZATION, THEIR CONNECTIONS WITH CUSTOMERS AND COMPETITORS, AND POTENTIAL CHANNELS FOR INSIGHTS.

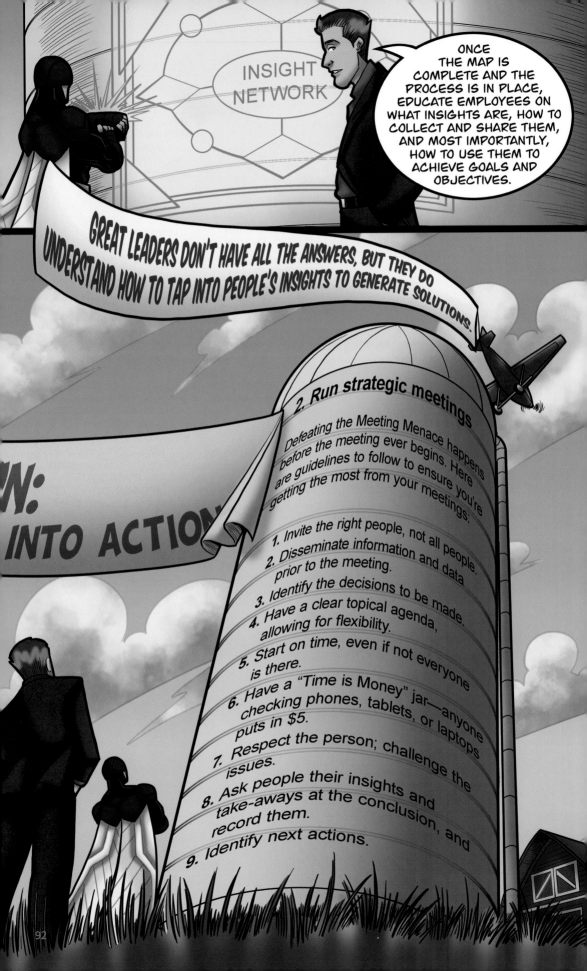

97

IF IT ISN'T MY OLD FRIEND, *STRATEGYMAN.*

I MISSED YOU AT *BLOCKBUSTER VIDEO* WHEN *NETFLIX* OFFERED TO SELL THEMSELVES FOR A MEAGER *$50 MILLION* AND BLOCKBUSTER OPTED NOT TO BUY.

AND AGAIN, WHEN *CIRCUIT CITY'S* LEADERS MOVED INTO UNRELATED BUSINESSES, INCLUDING CARMAX AND DIVX, A QUICKLY OBSOLETE VIDEO RENTAL SYSTEM.

DECISIONS—OR THE *LACK* THEREOF—CAN MAKE OR BREAK A STRATEGY.

WHO, OR *WHAT,* ARE *YOU?*

HE'S BEEN HERE THE ENTIRE TIME. HE EXERTS AN EVIL INFLUENCE ON YOUR DECISION-MAKING PROCESS. HIS METHODS ARE SUBTLE BUT DEVILISHLY DESTRUCTIVE.

WHERE ARE MY MANNERS? I'M THE INCORRIGIBLE, IRRESISTIBLE, *DECISION DEMON,* AT YOUR SERVICE.

OH *PLEASE,* STRATEGYMAN. YOU'RE MAKING ME *BLUSH.*

YOU LIKE THE DECISIONS YOU'VE MADE, DON'T YOU?

IT SEEMS LIKE SOME OF THESE WEREN'T DECISIONS AT ALL BUT US FALLING BACK INTO OLD HABITS.

NO, NO, *NO,* MY DEAR LADY. A DECISION YOU *EVADE* IS A DECISION *MADE.*

BUT CHANGE DOESN'T ALWAYS WORK OUT.

NO, BUT THE COMPETITIVE LANDSCAPE HAS SHIFTED, AND WITH IT, CUSTOMERS' EXPECTATIONS ON VALUE.

FIFTH, YOU PROJECTED A SALES FORECAST ON PURELY ANECDOTAL DATA.

SIXTH, YOU USED CONFIRMATION BIAS TO ASSUME THE CONVERSION RATE WOULD BE HIGHER THAN NORMAL.

SEVENTH, THE HALO EFFECT MADE YOU ASSUME THAT THE POSITIVE EFFECT OF PRICE INCREASES IN THE PAST WOULD CARRY OVER TO FUTURE DECISIONS.

EIGHT WAS MOST LIKELY US ANCHORING OUR DECISION ON WHAT HAS WORKED FOR US IN THE PAST IN TERMS OF CUSTOMER CONVERSIONS AND PRICE INCREASES.

NOT SURE WHAT NUMBER NINE COULD BE.

101

MULTI-TASKINATORS = MULTITASKING (DOING SEVERAL THINGS AT ONCE) + TERMINATOR (DESTROYER)

- **MULTITASKING IS AN UNCEASING AND QUIETLY DESTRUCTIVE FORCE FOR MANY.**

Smartphones are a common tool Multi-taskinators use to distract us. Studies show people check their smartphones, on average, every 6½ minutes, or roughly 150 times a day![1] This constant shuffling back and forth between tasks has become the norm and is assumed by many to be a hallmark of highly productive people. Unfortunately, it's not.

CLIFFORD NASS' STUDIES FROM STANFORD UNIVERSITY SUGGEST THAT MANAGERS WHO CONTINUALLY SHIFT BETWEEN MULTIPLE TASKS DO NOT MANAGE THOSE TASKS AS WELL AS THOSE WHO FOCUS ON ONE THING AT A TIME:[2]

85%

- Productive
○ Unproductive
- Uncategorized

WORKER 1 HAD 277 SWITCHES OF TASKS DURING THE DAY AND WAS 85% PRODUCTIVE AND ONLY 7% UNPRODUCTIVE.

33% 63%

WORKER 2 HAD 496 SWITCHES OF TASKS DURING THE DAY AND WAS ONLY 33% PRODUCTIVE AND A WHOPPING 63% UNPRODUCTIVE.[3]

AH, YES, AND THERE'S DATA TO SHOW THAT WHEN PEOPLE SWITCH BETWEEN TASKS, THEY TAKE UP TO 30% LONGER TO COMPLETE THEM AND MAKE TWICE AS MANY ERRORS AS THOSE THAT DON'T SWITCH.[4]

MULTITASKING MAY MAKE YOU *FEEL* MORE PRODUCTIVE, BUT YOU'RE ONLY FOOLING YOURSELF. IT'S ACTUALLY *HURTING* YOUR OVERALL PERFORMANCE MUCH MORE THAN YOU IMAGINE.

"The very act of seeking out new information has been found to trigger the release of the pleasure-producing chemical dopamine in our brains. We're rewarded for hunting and gathering data, even if the data are trivial, and so we become compulsive in checking the networked gadgets we carry around with us all day."

—*Harvard Business School Dean Nitin Nohria, on why we multitask*[5]

"Decision effectiveness and financial results correlated at a 95% confidence level. Companies that are most effective at decision-making and execution generated average total shareholder returns nearly six percentage points higher than those of other firms."

—*Blenko, Mankins, and Rogers*[6]

Time can be classified as either:

monochromic, meaning we perform one task within a given period,

or **polychromic**, meaning we perform multiple tasks in a given period.

THERE'S A STRAIGHTFORWARD, ALBEIT CHALLENGING, SOLUTION TO MULTITASKING: CARVING OUT BLOCKS OF TIME IN YOUR SCHEDULE.

WHETHER INTERRUPTIONS ARE SELF-IMPOSED, SUCH AS CHECKING YOUR PHONE OR TABLET FOR TEXTS AND EMAILS, OR EXTERNAL FROM BOSSES AND COLLEAGUES, IT'S IMPORTANT TO FEND OFF SACROSANCT PERIODS FREE OF THEM.

IF YOU DON'T CARVE OUT BLOCKS OF TIME TO MAKE PROGRESS ON IMPORTANT INITIATIVES, THEIR ATTAINMENT WILL TAKE CONSIDERABLY LONGER. YOU MAY EVEN FIND YOU MAKE NO PROGRESS AT ALL.

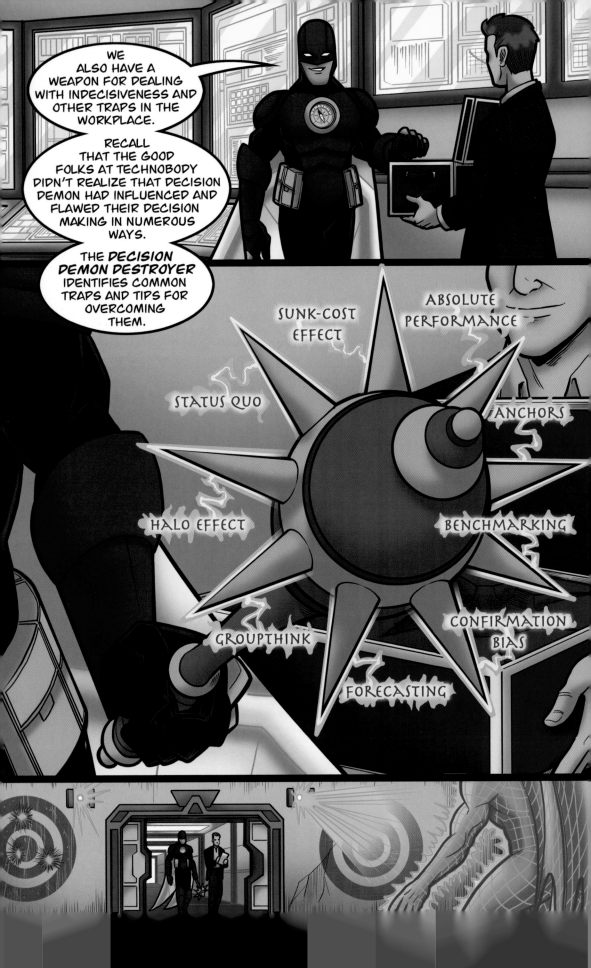

**TRAP:
Absolute
Performance**

*Forgetting that
performance is
always relative to
the competition*

**How to defeat
Absolute
Performance:**

☀ Measure your
progress against other
organizations.

☀ Create a system to
monitor and record
business intelligence
(market, customers,
competitors, and the
company), and make it
available to managers.

☀ When internal factors
such as sales force or
R&D are declared
strengths, ask how they
stack up against the
best in the industry.

**TRAP:
Anchors**

*Giving initial
information or
impressions a
disproportionate
amount of weight*

**How to defeat
Anchors:**

☀ Create an open mind
by actively considering
the range of starting
points available, not
just the anchor point.

☀ View the issue from
different frames (e.g.,
marketing manager
should seek views of
HR, sales, and
operations managers).

☀ Identify anchors as
soon as they appear,
and call them out
mentally and physically
(on paper/PC/flip
chart) so everyone is
aware of their presence.

**TRAP:
Benchmarking**

*Taking an
incomplete view of
what exactly is at
the root of another
firm's success*

**How to defeat
Benchmarking:**

☀ Identify what
exactly is being
benchmarked.

☀ Describe the
context in which the
benchmarked practice
is occurring, and
compare it to your
situation.

☀ Identify the strategy
ecosystem of the
benchmarked practice
and the relationships
involved in the
system.

**TRAP:
Confirmation Bias**

Seeking out data and information to support what one believes while discounting evidence to the contrary

How to defeat Confirmation Bias:

☼ Record the evidence for each position in a ledger format to enhance an objective view.

☼ Acknowledge the underpinnings of your reason for taking a position, and consider the opposite motivations.

☼ Bring in someone to present the other positions to provide a fresh perspective.

**TRAP:
Forecasting**

Being overconfident, giving prominence to what is first recalled, and using an average when a range of numbers would be more precise

How to defeat Forecasting:

☼ *Overconfidence:* Use a range with the extremes as bookends to estimate a spectrum of values.

☼ *Recollection:* Identify the data or facts for the events to ground your thinking in an objective base.

☼ *Averages:* Use a range of numbers whenever possible versus a single figure.

**TRAP:
Groupthink**

The effect of a homogenous group of people with little influence from outside sources and a high level of pressure to conform

How to defeat Groupthink:

☼ Assign one person in the group to play devil's advocate and take the opposite position of the majority.

☼ Utilize an external resource to ensure objectivity and divergent opinions.

☼ Bring in people from other functional areas (marketing, R&D, IT, HR) to offer fresh perspectives.

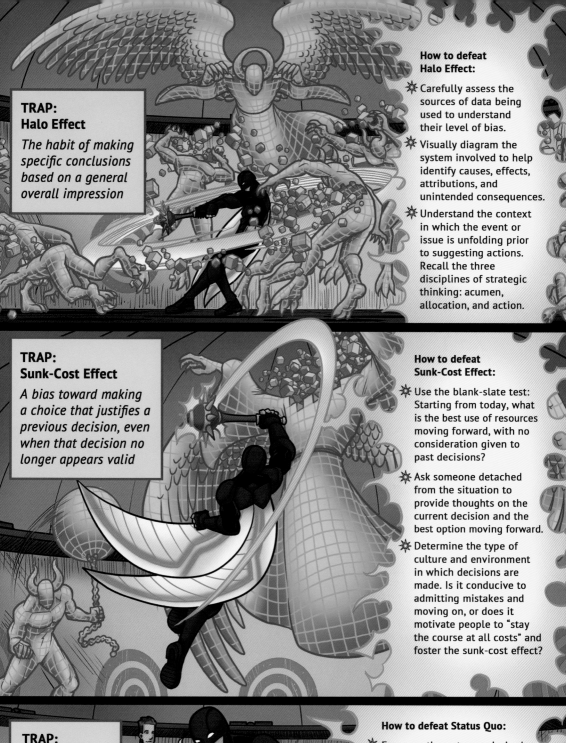

TRAP:
Halo Effect

The habit of making specific conclusions based on a general overall impression

How to defeat Halo Effect:

☀ Carefully assess the sources of data being used to understand their level of bias.

☀ Visually diagram the system involved to help identify causes, effects, attributions, and unintended consequences.

☀ Understand the context in which the event or issue is unfolding prior to suggesting actions. Recall the three disciplines of strategic thinking: acumen, allocation, and action.

TRAP:
Sunk-Cost Effect

A bias toward making a choice that justifies a previous decision, even when that decision no longer appears valid

How to defeat Sunk-Cost Effect:

☀ Use the blank-slate test: Starting from today, what is the best use of resources moving forward, with no consideration given to past decisions?

☀ Ask someone detached from the situation to provide thoughts on the current decision and the best option moving forward.

☀ Determine the type of culture and environment in which decisions are made. Is it conducive to admitting mistakes and moving on, or does it motivate people to "stay the course at all costs" and foster the sunk-cost effect?

TRAP:
Status Quo

Affinity for the existing state or condition

How to defeat Status Quo:

☀ Focus on the outcome desired, and use that as a measurement between the status quo and other alternatives.

☀ Examine the actual changes that would need to be made to abandon the status quo, as the reality is often less painful than imagined.

☀ Explore a range of alternatives outside the status quo to provide a full picture of the potential courses of action and their accompanying benefits.

GREAT WORK, STRATEGYMAN. LET'S BRING THIS WEAPON TO THE FOLKS AT TECHNOBODY.

109

SHAME ON ME FOR NOT NOTICING HOW BLOATED THE PLAN WAS GETTING. SOMETIMES, I GUESS I FEEL SAFER IF THERE'S MORE IN IT, SO PEOPLE CAN'T SECOND-GUESS AS MUCH IF WE DON'T HIT OUR NUMBERS.

WHICH EXPLAINS WHY WE HAVE EVERY POSSIBLE TACTIC LISTED, EVEN THOUGH WE KNOW WE'LL NEVER DO THEM ALL.

WELL, NOW THAT WE'VE NOTICED, MAYBE WE CAN DO A BETTER JOB OF CREATING A MORE CONCISE PLAN THAT PEOPLE WILL ACTUALLY USE TO DRIVE THEIR DAILY ACTIVITIES.

THAT REMINDS ME: HAVE YOU THOUGHT ANY MORE ABOUT INNOVATARA'S RIDDLE ON HOW TO FIND THE INSIGHTRON?

"WHAT'S THERE, BUT YOU CAN'T SEE IT, CAN HELP YOU OR HURT YOU, AND TYPICALLY ACTS LIKE A BIRTHDAY?"

A COUPLE OF IDEAS HAVE COME TO MIND, BUT I NEED TO DO A LITTLE MORE WORK, AND WE'RE RUNNING OUT OF *TIME*.

NOT TO MENTION WE'LL ALL BE OUT LOOKING FOR *JOBS*.

IF WE DON'T FIND THE INSIGHTRON SOON, IT SOUNDS LIKE OUR STRATEGIC PLAN WON'T SURVIVE THE MONTH AND WE WON'T BE ABLE TO COMPLETE THE E-SKIN SUIT.

I WONDER IF THE GUEST KEYNOTE SPEAKER WILL BE ABLE TO SHED ANY LIGHT ON THESE ISSUES. AFTER ALL, HE *IS* A DOCTOR...

NOT HAVING A SOLID STRATEGY DEVELOPMENT PROCESS IN PLACE ENSURES ONE OF TWO OUTCOMES: NO PLAN OR A PLAN THAT'S NOT CLEAR AND CONCISE ON THE KEYS TO WINNING IN YOUR MARKET.

EITHER WAY, THE RESULTING LACK OF DIRECTION MANIFESTS ITSELF IN A LOSS OF CONFIDENCE IN THE COMPANY'S FUTURE AND AN UNDISCIPLINED LACK OF FOCUS ON WHICH OPPORTUNITIES TO PURSUE.

I'D LIKE AN UNFOCUSED PLAN, PLEASE.

DR. YES AND MEGALO-PLAN FEED ON PLANS LIKE THOSE.

I REMEMBER THAT FORMER CEO OF CIRCUIT CITY, ALAN WURTZEL, IN HIS BOOK GOOD TO GREAT TO GONE, CITED THAT THE COMPANY'S LACK OF ATTENTION TO STRATEGIC PLANNING HAD RUN IT INTO THE DITCH.[3] IS THAT THE KIND OF THING YOU'RE REFERRING TO?

WHAT CAN I GET YOU ALL FOR LUNCH?

EXACTLY. AND REMEMBER THAT LACK OF ATTENTION CAN ALSO COME IN THE FORM OF LACK OF DISCIPLINE.

LOADING UP A PLAN WITH NON-ESSENTIAL DATA, LAUNDRY LISTS OF TACTICS, AND EXTRANEOUS SLIDES THAT DON'T CONTRIBUTE INSIGHTS TO THE PLAN ALL DEMONSTRATE POOR DISCIPLINE.

A survey of nearly 5,000 senior executives showed that more than 50% didn't think they had a winning strategy in place.[4]

If you show up in the morning and don't believe in your strategy, you may want to start buying your competitor's stock.

THIS MEGALO-PLAN MENTALITY CLUTTERS YOUR THINKING, MUDDIES THE STRATEGIC DIRECTION, AND DESTROYS THE ALL-IMPORTANT CLARITY THAT A GOOD PLAN DELIVERS.

I'LL TAKE THIS, PLEASE.

Lava Cake for Two
with Ice Cream, Whipped Cre[am]
Sprinkles, and Cherrie[s]

OOOOKAY. THANK YOU... MA'AM?

THANK *YOU!*

WHILE MEGALO-PLAN IS A BIG, TANGIBLE ISSUE, DR. YES CAN EXIST SURREPTITIOUSLY, REMAINING UNDETECTED IN THE NORMAL COURSE OF BUSINESS.

UNLIKE FIRE DRILLER, HE ISN'T A RAUCOUS, ADRENALINE-FEASTING BEING THAT DOMINATES PEOPLE'S ATTENTION. HE OFTEN OPERATES IN THE SMALL DECISIONS THAT GUIDE OUR DAILY ACTIVITIES. HE THRIVES ON PEOPLE'S UNWILLINGNESS TO ROCK THE BOAT.

FOR MOST OF US, IT'S EASIER TO SAY YES THAN TO SAY NO, ESPECIALLY TO OUR COLLEAGUES' REQUESTS.

UNFORTUNATELY, PURSUING ALL POTENTIAL OPPORTUNITIES, AGREEING TO ATTEND MEETINGS OR TELECONFERENCES WHERE THERE AREN'T NEW INSIGHTS, AND SAYING YES TO TASKS THAT AREN'T OUR RESPONSIBILITY DILUTE OUR TIME, WASTE OUR TALENT, AND LOWER MORALE.

Jerry Greenfield, cofounder of Ben & Jerry's ice cream empire, said the following when asked what advice he would give himself if he could go back to the early years: "I think we could have been more selective in chasing opportunities. We just felt so much pressure to go after so many different things when we started growing: new markets, new products. It's hard to do things well when you're trying to do so much so quickly."[5]

I'LL TAKE THIS, PLEASE.

Fish Tacos

AND YOU, MISS?

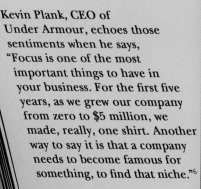

Kevin Plank, CEO of Under Armour, echoes those sentiments when he says, "Focus is one of the most important things to have in your business. For the first five years, as we grew our company from zero to $5 million, we made, really, one shirt. Another way to say it is that a company needs to become famous for something, to find that niche."[6]

I'LL JUST HAVE THE GRILLED SALMON, THANKS.

WE HAVE SOMETHING FOR YOU.

FIVE TECHNIQUES YOU CAN USE TO VANQUISH MEGALO-PLAN AND DR. YES AND SAVE TECHNOBODY'S STRATEGIC PLAN.

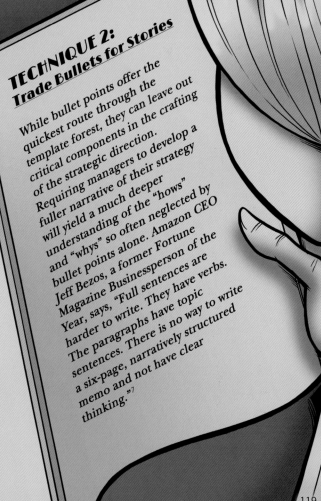

THINKTION:
Transforming Thinking into Action

TECHNIQUE 1:
Stimulate New Thinking

The reason most plans are nothing more than a compilation of last year's updated goals and tactics is because no new thinking takes place. Identify and select questions, tools, and frameworks to productively facilitate thinking and dialogue about the key business issues. Then visually capture the important insights from the discussion using the appropriate strategic thinking tools.

TECHNIQUE 2:
Trade Bullets for Stories

While bullet points offer the quickest route through the template forest, they can leave out critical components in the crafting of the strategic direction. Requiring managers to develop a fuller narrative of their strategy will yield a much deeper understanding of the "hows" and "whys" so often neglected by bullet points alone. Amazon CEO Jeff Bezos, a former Fortune Magazine Businessperson of the Year, says, "Full sentences are harder to write. They have verbs. The paragraphs have topic sentences. There is no way to write a six-page, narratively structured memo and not have clear thinking."[7]

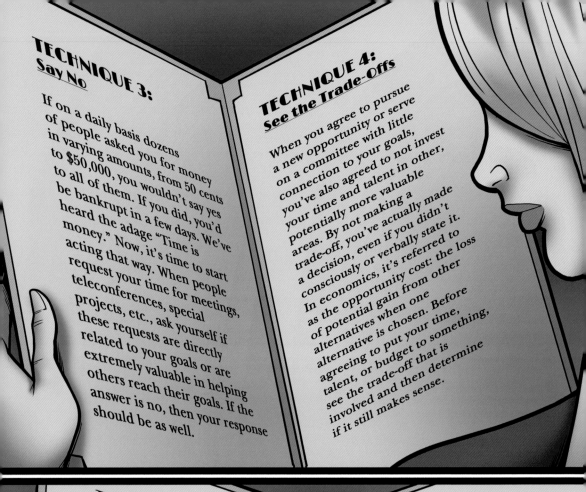

TECHNIQUE 3:
Say No

If on a daily basis dozens of people asked you for money in varying amounts, from 50 cents to $50,000, you wouldn't say yes to all of them. If you did, you'd be bankrupt in a few days. We've heard the adage "Time is money." Now, it's time to start acting that way. When people request your time for meetings, teleconferences, special projects, etc., ask yourself if these requests are directly related to your goals or are extremely valuable in helping others reach their goals. If the answer is no, then your response should be as well.

TECHNIQUE 4:
See the Trade-Offs

When you agree to pursue a new opportunity or serve on a committee with little connection to your goals, you've also agreed to not invest your time and talent in other, potentially more valuable areas. By not making a trade-off, you've actually made a decision, even if you didn't consciously or verbally state it. In economics, it's referred to as the opportunity cost: the loss of potential gain from other alternatives when one alternative is chosen. Before agreeing to put your time, talent, or budget to something, see the trade-off that is involved and then determine if it still makes sense.

TECHNIQUE 5:
Use Templates to Share Insights

Templates aren't inherently evil. It's their misuse and overuse that have given them a bad reputation. Selecting a handful of templates that effectively communicate insights regarding important business issues is part of planning. Accompanying each template should be the key insights drawn from that template. If you have templates in your plan that don't produce a "so what?" or "take-away," then pull them out. As former Intel CEO Andy Grove said, "The model doesn't tell you what the answer is. But it gave us a common language and a common way to frame the problem, so that we could reach consensus around a counterintuitive course of action."[8]

WEAPON
The Trade-Off Matrix

	Increase
Eliminate	Strategy conversations
Manual reports	Think time
	Create
Decrease	Insight journal
Review meetings	Strategy champions
Email	

Use this weapon to disable Megalo-Plan and Dr. Yes. The Trade-Off Matrix provides an effective way to change your team's behaviors to become more strategic. The four quadrants represent future behaviors with regards to your resources. As you review how you and your team currently invest your resources (time, talent, budget), the Trade-Off Matrix stimulates thinking on the activities, areas, and items you'd recommend to "Eliminate," "Decrease," "Increase," and "Create."

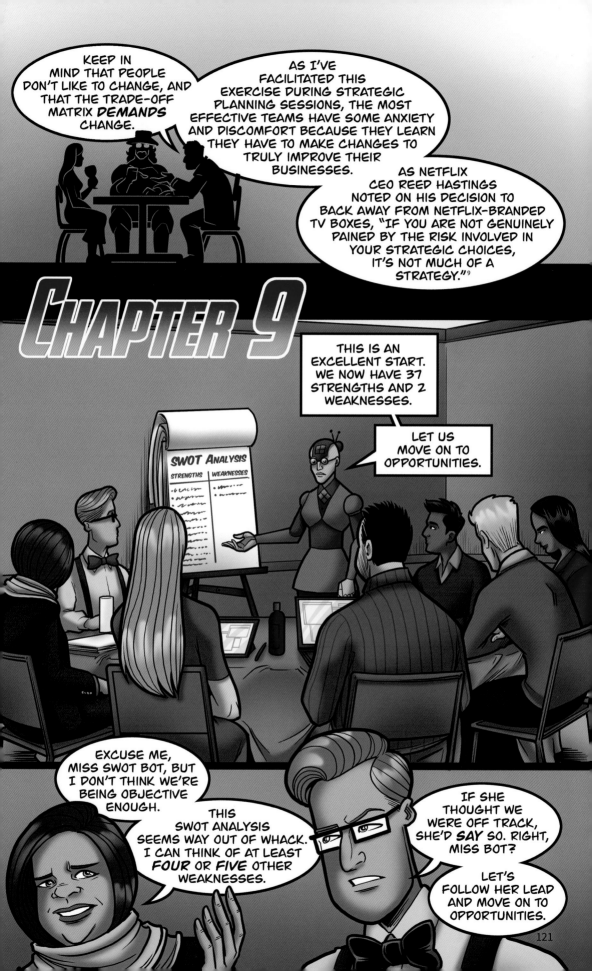

KEEP IN MIND THAT PEOPLE DON'T LIKE TO CHANGE, AND THAT THE TRADE-OFF MATRIX **DEMANDS** CHANGE.

AS I'VE FACILITATED THIS EXERCISE DURING STRATEGIC PLANNING SESSIONS, THE MOST EFFECTIVE TEAMS HAVE SOME ANXIETY AND DISCOMFORT BECAUSE THEY LEARN THEY HAVE TO MAKE CHANGES TO TRULY IMPROVE THEIR BUSINESSES.

AS NETFLIX CEO REED HASTINGS NOTED ON HIS DECISION TO BACK AWAY FROM NETFLIX-BRANDED TV BOXES, "IF YOU ARE NOT GENUINELY PAINED BY THE RISK INVOLVED IN YOUR STRATEGIC CHOICES, IT'S NOT MUCH OF A STRATEGY."[9]

CHAPTER 9

THIS IS AN EXCELLENT START. WE NOW HAVE 37 STRENGTHS AND 2 WEAKNESSES.

LET US MOVE ON TO OPPORTUNITIES.

SWOT ANALYSIS

STRENGTHS | WEAKNESSES

EXCUSE ME, MISS SWOT BOT, BUT I DON'T THINK WE'RE BEING OBJECTIVE ENOUGH.

THIS SWOT ANALYSIS SEEMS WAY OUT OF WHACK. I CAN THINK OF AT LEAST **FOUR** OR **FIVE** OTHER WEAKNESSES.

IF SHE THOUGHT WE WERE OFF TRACK, SHE'D **SAY** SO. RIGHT, MISS BOT?

LET'S FOLLOW HER LEAD AND MOVE ON TO OPPORTUNITIES.

LATER THAT DAY...

STRENGTHS AND WEAKNESSES ARE MADE UP OF FACTORS OVER WHICH THE GROUP HAS GREATER RELATIVE CONTROL.

Factors that may make up strengths and weaknesses:
• Skill sets
• Resources (people, money, time)
• Knowledge base
• Processes and systems, including operational and customer-facing
• Staffing practices
• Brand
• Values
• Culture

Opportunities and threats are made up of those factors over which the organization has influence but not control. These factors include:
• Overall demand
• Competitor activity
• Market saturation
• Government policies
• Economic conditions
• Social, cultural, and ethical developments
• Technological developments

THE SWOT ALIGNMENT MODEL ALIGNS THE INTERNAL CAPABILITIES —STRENGTHS AND WEAKNESSES—WITH THE EXTERNAL POSSIBILITIES—OPPORTUNITIES AND THREATS—TO METHODICALLY DEVELOP POTENTIAL STRATEGIES.

IT TAKES THE ESSENCE OF THE SWOT ANALYSIS AND ANSWERS THE QUESTION, "SO WHAT?" IN OTHER WORDS, BASED ON THE STRENGTHS, WEAKNESSES, OPPORTUNITIES, AND THREATS IDENTIFIED, WHAT SHOULD YOU DO?

THE BIGGEST KNOCK ON SWOT ANALYSIS IS THAT WE TYPICALLY DON'T DO ANYTHING WITH IT. THE SWOT ALIGNMENT FRAMEWORK ENABLES YOU TO MOVE FROM SWOT ANALYSIS TO STRATEGIES FOR YOUR BUSINESS.

SWOT Alignment Model

I CREATED A MOCK SWOT ALIGNMENT MODEL FOR TECHNOBODY'S BRAIN BIN 2 PRODUCT.

TO CONSTRUCT THE SWOT ALIGNMENT MODEL, LIST THE STRENGTHS, WEAKNESSES, OPPORTUNITIES, AND THREATS IN THEIR RESPECTIVE BOXES.

THEN CREATE POTENTIAL STRATEGIES BY METHODICALLY ALIGNING THE STRENGTHS AND OPPORTUNITIES, STRENGTHS AND THREATS, WEAKNESSES AND OPPORTUNITIES, AND WEAKNESSES AND THREATS IN THE APPROPRIATE BOXES. THIS MODEL SERVES AS AN EFFECTIVE EXERCISE AFTER A SWOT ANALYSIS...

...TO MOVE FROM THINKING TO ACTION.

NOW, WHAT'S THIS ABOUT THE BRAIN BIN 2 PRODUCT LAUNCH?

I'M HERE TO SEE THAT IT'S POORLY EXECUTED.

WHY WOULD YOU *DO* THAT?

BECAUSE I'M AN *EXECUTIONER.*

FIREFIGHTING · TOO MANY PRIORITIES · STATUS QUO

BUT, YOUR SWORD ISN'T EVEN *SHARP.*

GET OUT OF HERE, YOU *LOUT!* YOU'RE THE WORST EXECUTIONER I'VE EVER *SEEN.* YOUR BLADE IS A *DISGRACE!*

I WAS... ERM... *REASSIGNED* FROM PEOPLE TO PRODUCT LAUNCHES.

I'M GOOD AT THOSE.

THE EXECUTIONER WIELDS THREE COMMON STRATEGY EXECUTION ERRORS AND HAS PLANS TO USE THEM ON THE BRAIN BIN 2 LAUNCH.

FIREFIGHTING, TOO MANY PRIORITIES, *AND* THE STATUS QUO?

IT *DOES* SOUND FAMILIAR. WE'VE BEEN HAVING SOME OF THOSE ISSUES.

REALLY?!

I MAY JUST GET MY JOB BACK AFTER ALL!

HAVE TO GET THIS INFORMATION TO THE FOLKS AT TECHNOBODY.

THINKTION: TRANSFORMING THINKING INTO ACTION

RESEARCH FROM 25 DIFFERENT COMPANIES AND MORE THAN 500 MANAGERS AROUND THE WORLD REVEALS THAT FIREFIGHTING, TOO MANY PRIORITIES, AND CLINGING TO THE STATUS QUO ARE THREE OF THE GREATEST STRATEGY CHALLENGES.[2] HERE'S HOW TO RESPOND TO THEM:

FIREFIGHTING:
A Review from Chapter 3

REMEMBER FIRE DRILLER? HE SHOWED US THAT FIREFIGHTING HAPPENS WHEN PEOPLE STOP WORKING PURPOSEFULLY AND RUSH TO TAKE CARE OF SOMETHING THAT JUST POPPED UP. YOU CAN EXTINGUISH THE FIRE DRILL MENTALITY IN YOUR GROUP BY ANSWERING THE FOLLOWING FIVE QUESTIONS:

1. DO WE NEED TO ATTEND TO THIS?

2. DOES THIS FALL WITHIN OUR RESPONSIBILITIES?

3. WHO CAN HANDLE THIS MORE EFFICIENTLY?

4. HOW DID THIS FIRE START IN THE FIRST PLACE?

5. WHAT STEPS CAN WE TAKE TO PREVENT FUTURE OCCURRENCES?

TOO MANY PRIORITIES

A PRIORITY IS SOMETHING THAT IS HIGHER IN IMPORTANCE AND GIVEN SPECIAL ATTENTION.[3] CONSIDER WHAT YOU'VE DEVOTED YOUR TIME TO THIS WEEK. WERE THOSE THINGS PRIORITIES? OR WERE THEY SIMPLY RANDOM ITEMS ON THE ACTIVITY CONVEYOR BELT? ONE ROOT CAUSE OF A LACK OF PRIORITIES IS NOT HAVING CLEAR GOALS AND STRATEGIES IN PLACE. CLEAR GOALS AND STRATEGIES ACT AS A FILTER TO ELIMINATE TASKS THAT DON'T WORK TOWARD THEIR ENDS. CLEAR GOALS AND STRATEGIES ALSO ILLUMINATE THOSE THINGS THAT CONTRIBUTE THE MOST TO THEIR ATTAINMENT.

AN EFFECTIVE TOOL FOR INSTILLING THE DISCIPLINE TO PRIORITIZE IS A CHECKLIST. AS DR. ATUL GAWANDE, PROFESSOR, SURGEON, AND AUTHOR, WROTE, "CHECKLISTS REMIND US OF THE MINIMUM NECESSARY STEPS AND MAKE THEM EXPLICIT. THEY NOT ONLY OFFER THE POSSIBILITY OF VERIFICATION BUT ALSO INSTILL A KIND OF DISCIPLINE OF HIGHER PERFORMANCE. CHECKLISTS PROVIDE A KIND OF COGNITIVE NET. THEY CATCH MENTAL FLAWS INHERENT IN ALL OF US—FLAWS OF MEMORY AND ATTENTION AND THOROUGHNESS."[4]

HERE'S AN EXAMPLE OF A PRIORITY CHECKLIST:

☐ THE TOP THREE TO FIVE GOALS AND THEIR STRATEGIES ARE CLEAR.

☐ A FULL SPECTRUM OF ACTIVITIES TO SUPPORT THE GOALS AND STRATEGIES HAVE BEEN IDENTIFIED.

☐ EACH POTENTIAL ACTIVITY HAS BEEN EVALUATED FOR PROBABILITY OF ACHIEVEMENT.

☐ EACH POTENTIAL ACTIVITY HAS BEEN EVALUATED FOR IMPACT ON THE BUSINESS GOALS.

☐ ONE TO THREE ACTIVITIES HAVE BEEN SELECTED AS PRIORITIES.

☐ THE "WHY" BEHIND THE CHOSEN PRIORITIES HAS BEEN SHARED.

☐ THE ONE TO THREE ACTIVITIES HAVE BEEN COMMUNICATED AS PRIORITIES.

☐ METRICS/MILESTONES TO GAUGE PROGRESS HAVE BEEN IDENTIFIED FOR EACH PRIORITY.

☐ A PERIODIC PRIORITIES REVIEW IS SCHEDULED.

STATUS QUO

New strategies require new behaviors. Once the excitement of the new strategies has worn off, the reality of having to change behavior sets in. This change in behavior can include new responsibilities, relationships, structures, processes, and activities. The implementation of these new things necessitates the letting go of old things. And those old things may be things we liked. But, as Walt Disney Company CEO Robert Iger said, "The riskiest thing Disney can do is just maintain the status quo."[5]

As human beings, our response to loss is more extreme than our response to gain. Consequently, when we're faced with a situation in which something will potentially be taken away (e.g., head count, geography, budget, etc.), our default response is risk-aversion and to bail on the priorities and their requisite trade-offs. We mistakenly assume the status quo is the safer bet.

To actively move out of a status quo mindset, use the following techniques where appropriate:

1. Write down your top three goals. Then ask, "Does the path of the status quo provide us with the best opportunity to achieve these?" If not, explore other options.

2. Discuss the actual changes required to move away from the status quo. Are the changes possible? What steps would you need to take to enact these changes?

3. Compile a list of the options outside the status quo and the benefits of each. Then compare this range of alternatives and their benefits with those of the status quo. Now, which appears more attractive?

IF TECHNOBODY'S CURRENT STRATEGIC PLAN IS MORE THAN TWO SLIDES OR PAGES, THERE'S A GOOD CHANCE THEY DON'T REALLY USE IT.

AND IF THEY'RE NOT USING THE PLAN TO DRIVE THEIR DAILY ACTIVITIES, THEY MAY AS WELL NOT HAVE ONE AT ALL.

ONE OF THE BIG GAPS I'VE IDENTIFIED IN ORGANIZATIONS OF ALL SIZES IS BETWEEN THE PLAN IN THE BINDER OR POWERPOINT DECK AND WHAT PEOPLE ARE DOING ON A DAILY BASIS.

TO BRIDGE THAT GAP, I DEVELOPED A TOOL CALLED THE STRATEGYPRINT.®

THE STRATEGYPRINT IS A TWO-PAGE BLUEPRINT OF A BUSINESS.

PAGE 1 CONTAINS KEY INSIGHTS ON THE FOUR AREAS OF ANY BUSINESS: MARKET, CUSTOMERS, COMPETITORS, AND COMPANY.

PAGE 2 CONTAINS AN ACTION PLAN, TYPICALLY CONSISTING OF GOALS, OBJECTIVES, STRATEGIES, TACTICS, AND METRICS.

IT IS IN THESE TWO PAGES THAT TECHNOBODY CAN DISTILL THE ESSENCE OF THEIR BUSINESS.

THEY CAN ALSO USE IT TO STAY ON POINT AND EFFECTIVELY COMMUNICATE THEIR FOCUS WITH OTHER MEMBERS OF THE ORGANIZATION OR BOARD OF DIRECTORS.

TECHNOBODY STRATEGYPRINT®

MARKET STATE & TRENDS
- Market growth is 16%
- Uncertain future of AI applications
- Longer contract cycles with accounts

CUSTOMERS
- National Football League contract coming up for bid
- National Hockey League looking to renegotiate
- New president for Major League Lacrosse
- New guidelines for student-athlete safety by NCAA
- American Youth Football having issues with Costazon Head Helmet

COMPETITION: COSTAZON

Strengths: Low cost structure, ease of use, comfort   Weaknesses: R&D, field sales force resources, product recall

Capabilities: Public company—access to capital, sales-driven culture, outsourced customer service

Activities: Targeted youth program education, promotion and sponsorship of extreme sports

Strategy: Judo approach—turn TechnoBody technology advantage into "too expensive"

COMPANY

STRENGTHS	WEAKNESSES	OPPORTUNITIES	THREATS
- Connectivity platform with future E-Skin Suit - Favorable scientific data on concussion prevention for Brain Bin 2 - Sales force coverage (2 reps for every 1 Costazon rep)	- Silos causing misalignment - Lack of product education materials for different groups - Incoherent strategic plan not directing activities	- Positive relationships with regional youth athletic orgs - Advocacy among neurologists - Coaches and players relying on tech for quicker decisions	- Costazon's Head Helmet clinical trials locking up potential customers - Restricted access to customers - Costazon's long-term contracts building access barriers

TECHNOBODY STRATEGYPRINT®

MISSION
Unite mind, body, and spirit in wearable technology.

VISION
Raise the consciousness of humanity

VALUES
1. Curiosity   2. Tenacity   3. Unity

GOALS
1. Launch Brain Bin 2
2. Sell services to Brain Bin customers
3. Enhance strategic thinking and planning skills

OBJECTIVES
1. Convert 75% of accounts from Brain Bin 1 to Brain Bin 2 in one year
2. Increase revenue-per-client by 20% through the sale of services by Q4
3. Improve profitability 10% by Q3

STRATEGIES
1. Develop a customer conversion program to facilitate product trial
2. Generate awareness of service offerings through consultative selling and needs assessment tools
3. Train managers on strategic thinking capabilities to improve resource allocation decisions

TACTICS
- Conversion materials
- Direct mail campaign
- Journal advertising

- Train sales force on service offerings
- Incentive program for service sales
- Direct mail campaign to service decision makers at hospital systems

- Assessment tools to baseline strategic thinking capabilities
- Conduct the Deep Dive Training System for mid-level managers
- Distribute Resource Allocation Calculators & train on use

TECHNOBODY CAN CUSTOMIZE THEIR STRATEGYPRINT SO THAT IT USES NOMENCLATURE THAT RESONATES WITH ITS TEAM.

THIS ENABLES THE TEAM TO ACTIVELY UPDATE THEIR STRATEGYPRINTS ON A MONTHLY BASIS.

THE BEAUTY OF THIS TOOL IS THAT IT CAN BE SCALED THROUGHOUT THE ORGANIZATION, RANGING FROM TERRITORY SALES REPRESENTATIVES UP THROUGH THE CEO AND ACROSS ALL FUNCTIONAL AREAS.

145

147

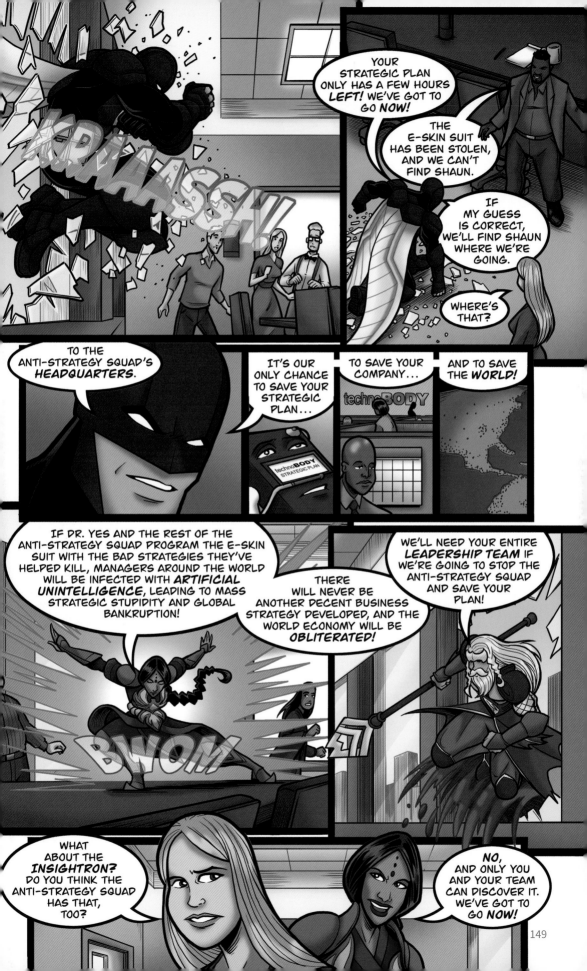

One study found that middle managers account for only 20% of the input into an organization's strategy.[1]

By allowing managers in different areas and levels to share their insights, senior leaders have a much greater chance for securing buy-in and commitment to the strategy once it's developed.

As strategic thinking shouldn't be an annual event, an ongoing channel for insight sharing should be continually cultivated. This encourages employees to continually mine their daily experiences for ideas to build their base of expertise and pass along to others.

IN ADDITION TO PROVIDING MANAGERS WITH THE OPPORTUNITY TO CONTRIBUTE THEIR INSIGHTS TO THE STRATEGY, IT'S EQUALLY IMPORTANT TO SHARE WITH EVERYONE WHY THE STRATEGY BEING PURSUED HAS BEEN CHOSEN.

PEOPLE DON'T HAVE TO AGREE WITH THE STRATEGY OR THE RATIONALE BEHIND THE WHY. THE IMPORTANT THING IS THEY WANT TO KNOW WHAT THE STRATEGY IS AND WHY.

IN ESSENCE, THEY NEED THE *BECAUSE*, AS IN "WE'RE DOING *X*, BECAUSE *Y*." THAT'S IT.

REASON FOR THE STRATEGY

WE'RE DOING *X*, BECAUSE *Y*.

Research in the social sciences shows that people are much more likely to fulfill a request if you simply give them a reason for doing it.

One study had a person standing in line waiting to make copies at a Xerox machine. If the participant asked the person ahead of them, "Excuse me, I have five pages. May I use the Xerox machine?" they were granted permission to go ahead 60% of the time. When the end of the request was changed to "May I use the Xerox machine because I'm in a rush?" the permission rate jumped to 94%.[2]

While the reason, "I'm in a rush," is fairly nebulous, it was prefaced by the magic word: **because**.

IF WE DON'T PROVIDE PEOPLE WITH THE REASON BEHIND THE STRATEGY, THEY'LL OFTEN MAKE ONE UP.

IN THE BEHAVIORAL SCIENCES, THIS IS REFERRED TO AS COUNTERFACTUAL THINKING. IN LAYMAN'S TERMS, COUNTERFACTUAL THINKING IS "SECOND-GUESSING." SECOND-GUESSING IS BORNE OUT OF PEOPLE'S DESIRE FOR UNDERSTANDING THE REASON WHY SOMETHING IS HAPPENING.

IN THE REALM OF BUSINESS STRATEGY, PEOPLE ARE MUCH LESS LIKELY TO "THROW THE LEADER UNDER THE BUS" IF THEIR INPUT WAS INCLUDED IN THE PROCESS AT SOME POINT AND THEY WERE THEN GIVEN A CLEAR STATEMENT OF STRATEGY AND WHY IT WAS CHOSEN.

TO GET MANAGERS TO TRULY UNDERSTAND AND APPLY STRATEGY IN THE COURSE OF THEIR DAILY WORK, YOU MUST SHARE WITH THEM THE WHY.

HHHHSSSSSSSSSSSSSS

WEAPON:
The Strategy Conversation Framework

HOW DID YOU DO THAT?

CRITICAL TO BOTH BUY-IN AND THE NURTURING OF CULTURE IS CONVERSATION.

WHILE A TREMENDOUS AMOUNT OF TALKING, TEXTING, AND EMAILING GOES ON EACH DAY, HOW MUCH OF IT IS TRULY PRODUCTIVE?

AS IT TURNS OUT, NOT MUCH. ONLY 32% OF ORGANIZATIONS TEACH THEIR MANAGERS HOW TO FACILITATE STRATEGY CONVERSATIONS.[3]

A TOOL FOR HAVING EFFECTIVE CONVERSATIONS THAT LEAD TO BUY-IN AND A HEALTHY CULTURE IS THE **STRATEGY CONVERSATION FRAMEWORK.**

HOW DOES IT WORK?

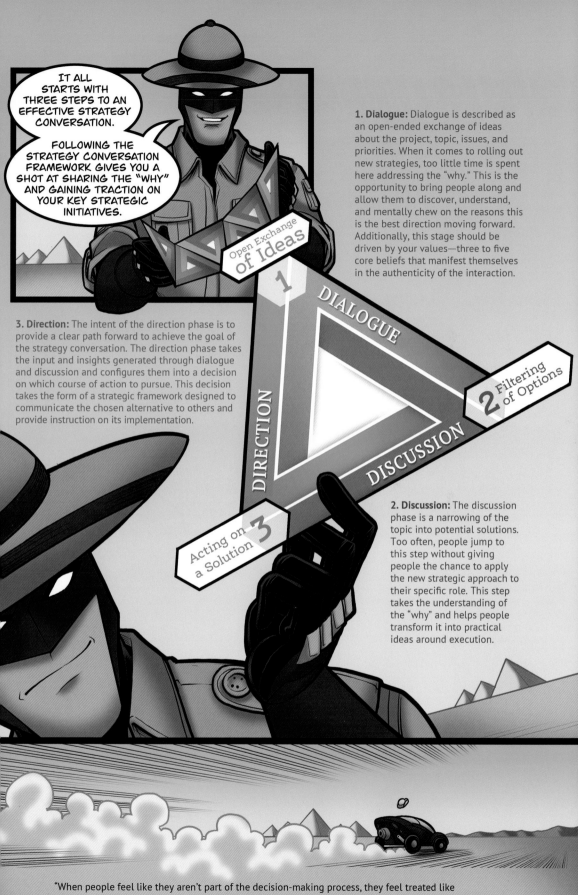

IT ALL STARTS WITH THREE STEPS TO AN EFFECTIVE STRATEGY CONVERSATION.

FOLLOWING THE STRATEGY CONVERSATION FRAMEWORK GIVES YOU A SHOT AT SHARING THE "WHY" AND GAINING TRACTION ON YOUR KEY STRATEGIC INITIATIVES.

1. Dialogue: Dialogue is described as an open-ended exchange of ideas about the project, topic, issues, and priorities. When it comes to rolling out new strategies, too little time is spent here addressing the "why." This is the opportunity to bring people along and allow them to discover, understand, and mentally chew on the reasons this is the best direction moving forward. Additionally, this stage should be driven by your values—three to five core beliefs that manifest themselves in the authenticity of the interaction.

3. Direction: The intent of the direction phase is to provide a clear path forward to achieve the goal of the strategy conversation. The direction phase takes the input and insights generated through dialogue and discussion and configures them into a decision on which course of action to pursue. This decision takes the form of a strategic framework designed to communicate the chosen alternative to others and provide instruction on its implementation.

Open Exchange of Ideas

1 DIALOGUE

DIRECTION

DISCUSSION

2 Filtering of Options

Acting on a Solution 3

2. Discussion: The discussion phase is a narrowing of the topic into potential solutions. Too often, people jump to this step without giving people the chance to apply the new strategic approach to their specific role. This step takes the understanding of the "why" and helps people transform it into practical ideas around execution.

"When people feel like they aren't part of the decision-making process, they feel treated like children, they feel resentful and you find examples of belligerent compliance. When people feel like they have had a say, like they have been empowered, you get collaboration and cooperation."[4]

—Ben Fried, CIO, Google

153

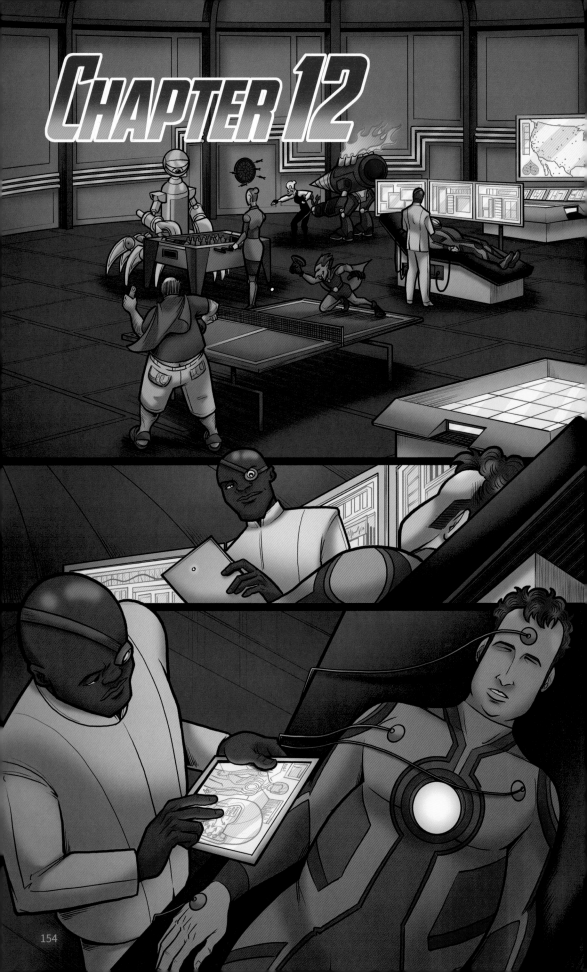

FRANK!
NO!

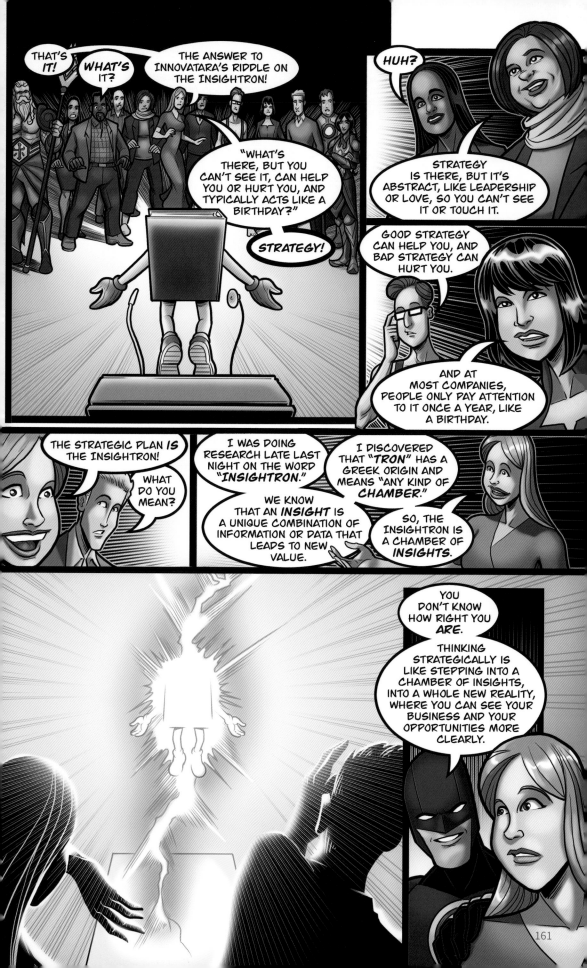

165

RICH HORWATH

When he isn't battling villains from the Anti-Strategy Squad, Rich Horwath is helping companies create an enterprise-wide capability in strategic thinking. Using the StrategyMobile, Rich has traveled around the world to facilitate strategy workshops for executive teams to set strategic direction and create competitive advantage. As CEO of the Strategic Thinking Institute, he has been a guide to more than 100,000 managers on their journey to develop strategic thinking and planning skills. Rich's academic service as a graduate school professor and real-world experience as a chief strategy officer have sharpened his strategy tools for the ongoing fight against bad strategy. To counter the Anti-Strategy Squad's strategycide campaign, Rich has spoken to managers at companies such as Google, FedEx, Intel, and L'Oréal, and has appeared on ABC, NBC, and FOX TV. A *New York Times* and *Wall Street Journal* bestselling author of seven books, he lives in Barrington Hills, IL, with his wife, two children, and StrategyMan occasionally crashing on the couch.

IF YOU'RE BATTLING VILLAINS FROM *THE ANTI-STRATEGY SQUAD* IN YOUR COMPANY, CONSIDER THE FOLLOWING ADDITIONAL RESOURCES.

StrategyMan Learning System

New research shows that the number-one most important skill for senior executives is strategic thinking. To rise in your organization, you need to be seen as strategic, not tactical. And to become skilled at anything, you need to practice it more than once a year. The same is true for strategy. The StrategyMan Learning System provides you with the opportunity to gain knowledge, practice skills, and evolve into a truly *strategic* leader. The online program offers an interactive and engaging forum to sharpen your strategy skills over time and to gain confidence, clarity of direction, and differentiation from others.

League of Strategists

A key factor in your growth and development is the ability to connect with and learn from others. This member-only online community of strategists provides a forum for you to build new skills, participate in Q&A, and share insights. You'll have exclusive access to new strategy content in the form of webinars, interviews, infographics, and many more innovative resources. Together, we can wage the war against bad strategy and share in our passion of thinking strategically.

Meta-Strategist Academy

For consultants and trainers interested in teaching the StrategyMan content to others, the Meta-Strategist Academy provides the tools, resources, and certification you need to deliver the StrategyMan Program with confidence. Research shows strategic thinking is the most important business skill for leaders. Your ability to teach this content to others can help companies of all sizes excel in their markets and significantly grow your business while positioning you as an expert.

Deep Dive: *The Proven Method for Building Strategy, Focusing Your Resources, and Taking Smart Action*

Book—Workshop—Learning Management System

Four studies on leadership all show that the number-one most valued skill in business today is strategic thinking. But only 3 out of every 10 managers are strategic. *Deep Dive* provides people at all levels with a road map to move from tactical to strategic to increase profits and competitive advantage. Building on the foundational principles of strategy, the book provides a simple framework and practical tools for thinking strategically on a daily basis to successfully achieve your goals.

Elevate: *The Three Disciplines of Advanced Strategic Thinking*

Book—Workshop—Learning Management System

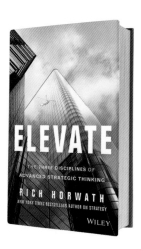

Research shows that only 25 percent of managers believe their companies are good at both strategy and innovation. It's no wonder, then, that poor strategy is the number-one cause of bankruptcy. Too often, strategy and innovation are approached separately. As the follow-up to *Deep Dive*, *Elevate* provides advanced content on strategic thinking and planning by helping leaders better prepare to fuse strategy and innovation into competitive advantage.

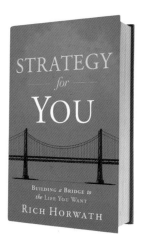

Strategy for You: *Building a Bridge to the Life You Want*

Book—Workshop—Learning Management System

In *Strategy for You*, Rich Horwath provides a five-step plan for building a bridge to the life you want. Using the foundational principles of business strategy, he lays out the five steps you can take to create a more fulfilling and successful life.

▷ **Visit www.strategyskills.com for more information.**

NOTES

Chapter 1

1. *The Strategic Mindset: Applying Strategic Thinking Skills for Organizational Success* (Strategic Thinking Institute and Human Capital Media Research Group, 2018), http://www.strategyskills.com/pdf/The-Strategic-Mindset.pdf.
2. Roger Martin, "The Execution Trap," *Harvard Business Review*, July–August 2010.
3. Christopher Dann, Matthew Le Merle, and Christopher Pencavel, "The Lesson of Lost Value," *strategy+business* 69 (Winter 2012).
4. Paul Carroll and Chunka Mui, "Seven Ways to Fail Big," *Harvard Business Review*, September 2008.
5. Dann, Le Merle, and Pencavel, "The Lesson of Lost Value."
6. *The Strategic Mindset.*

Chapter 2

1. Robert Safian, "Find Your Mission," *Fast Company*, November 2014.
2. B. H. Liddell Hart, *Strategy* (New York: Penguin Group, 1991).
3. Bob Thomas, *Walt Disney: An American Original* (New York: Simon & Schuster, 1994).
4. Ibid.

Chapter 3

1. Rich Horwath, *Elevate: The Three Disciplines of Advanced Strategic Thinking* (New York: John Wiley & Sons, 2014).
2. Michael Mankins, Chris Brahm, and Gregory Caimi, "Your Scarcest Resource," *Harvard Business Review*, May 2014.
3. "Clocking In," *Business Strategy Review* 4 (2011).
4. Frankki Bevins and Aaron De Smet, "Making time management the organization's priority," *McKinsey Quarterly*, January 2013.
5. Ibid.
6. Peter Bregman, "A personal approach to organizational time management," *McKinsey Quarterly*, January 2013.
7. "habit," *Merriam-Webster*, accessed May 15, 2017.
8. Ann Graybiel, "The Basal Ganglia and Chunking of Action Repertoires," *Neurobiology of Learning and Memory* 70, nos. 1–2 (July 1998): 119–36.

Chapter 4

1. Chris Zook and James Allen, *Repeatability* (Boston: Harvard Business Review Press, 2012).
2. Ed Catmull, "How Pixar Fosters Collective Creativity," *Harvard Business Review*, September 2008.
3. Michael Birshan, Emma Gibbs, and Kurt Strovink, "Rethinking the role of the strategist," *McKinsey Quarterly*, November 2014.
4. Stephen Hall, Dan Lovallo, and Reinier Musters, "How to put your money where your strategy is," *McKinsey Quarterly*, March 2012.

Chapter 5

1. Sam Grobart, "One Direction," *BusinessWeek*, September 19, 2013.
2. Duncan Simester, "Why Great New Products Fail," *MIT Sloan Management Review*, Spring 2016.
3. Daniel McGinn, "The Numbers in Jeff Bezos's Head," *Harvard Business Review*, November 2014.
4. Steve Hamm, "The Vacuum Man Takes On Wet Hands," *BusinessWeek*, July 2, 2007.

Chapter 6

1. Gillian Tett, *The Silo Effect* (New York: Simon & Schuster, 2015).
2. Ibid.
3. Mankins, Brahm, and Caimi, "Your Scarcest Resource."
4. Ibid.
5. Peter Bregman, *18 Minutes* (New York: Business Plus, 2011).
6. Katharina Herrmann, Asmus Komm, and Sven Smit, "Do you have the right leaders for your growth strategies?" *McKinsey Quarterly*, July 2011.
7. Chris Bradley, Martin Hirt, and Sven Smit, "Have You Tested Your Strategy Lately?" *McKinsey Quarterly*, January 2011.

Chapter 7

1. Scott Barry Kaufman and Carolyn Gregoire, *Wired to Create: Unraveling the Mysteries of the Creative Mind* (New York: Perigee, 2015).
2. Larry Rosen and Alexandra Samuel, "Conquering Digital Distraction," *Harvard Business Review*, June 2015.
3. HBR Staff, "The Multitasking Paradox," *Harvard Business Review*, March 2013.
4. Derek Dean and Caroline Webb, "Recovering from Information Overload," *McKinsey Quarterly*, January 2011.
5. Dominic Barton and Mark Wiseman, "Perspectives on the Long Term," *McKinsey Quarterly*, March 2015.
6. Marcia Blenko, Michael Mankins, and Paul Rogers, "The Decision-Driven Organization," *Harvard Business Review*, June 2010.

Chapter 8

1. Michael Birshan, Renee Dye, and Stephen Hall, "Creating more value with corporate strategy: McKinsey Global Survey results," *McKinsey&Company*, January 2011.
2. Doug Ross, "A new view of strategic leadership," *Strategy Magazine*, March 2007.
3. Alan Wurtzel, *Good to Great to Gone: The 60 Year Rise and Fall of Circuit City* (New York: Diversion Books, 2012).
4. Paul Leinwand and Cesare Maindari, "Creating a Strategy that Works," *strategy+business* 82 (Spring 2016).
5. J. D. Harrison, "Ben & Jerry's scrappy origins," *Chicago Tribune*, June 4, 2014.
6. Kevin Plank, "My Formula for Innovative Design," *Inc.*, July/August 2014.
7. Christian Bonilla, "The 3 Hardest Things You Need to Learn if You Want an Amazing Career," *Inc.*, November 2015.
8. Polly Labarre, "The Industrialized Revolution," *Fast Company*, November 2003.
9. Michael Copeland, "Reed Hastings: Leader of the Pack," *Fortune*, November 18, 2010.

Chapter 10

1. Gary Neilson, Karla Martin, and Elizabeth Powers, "The Secrets to Successful Strategy Execution," *Harvard Business Review*, June 2008.
2. Horwath, *Elevate: The Three Disciplines of Advanced Strategic Thinking*.
3. "priority," *Merriam-Webster*, accessed May 15, 2017.
4. Atul Gawande, *The Checklist Manifesto* (New York: Henry Holt and Company, 2009).
5. Bill George, "The Leadership Quality that Truly Separates Disney's Bob Iger From his Peers," *Fortune*, April 4, 2016.

Chapter 11

1. Fiona Czerniawska, "Executing Strategy: Lessons from Private Equity," *Strategy Magazine*, September 2007.
2. Ellen Langer, Arthur Blank, and Benzion Chanowitz, "The Mindlessness of Ostensibly Thoughtful Action: The Role of 'Placebic' Information in Interpersonal Interaction," *Journal of Personality and Social Psychology* 36, no. 6 (1978): 635–42.
3. *The Strategic Mindset*.
4. Steven Rosenbush, "When it Comes to IT, Google Thinks Differently," *Wall Street Journal*, October 20, 2014.

INDEX

INSIGHTS